MW00875693

The Edwardian Hotel Cookbook

The Edwardian Hotel Cookbook
Edited by Lee Lightfoot
Cover illustration by Tori Horner
Published by Black Ship Books
43 Melton Avenue
York, YO30 5QQ
North Yorkshire
United Kingdom

Copyright © 2012 Black Ship Books
Printed in the United Kingdom

UK ISBN 978-1481064972

10 9 8 7 6 5 4 3 2 1

Introduction

You hold in your hand a piece of history. I believe that Annie Leetham, the wife of prominent Yorkshire industrialist Sidney Leetham, conceived of this book as a precursor to the Elm Bank Hotel menu.

The original recipe book is dated two years before York's striking flour mill arose by Rowntree Wharf, Navigation Road. Leetham was known for this and several other mills, amongst the vanguard of milling technology in Britain at the time.

Sidney Leetham is also notable for a well-publicised redecoration of his Elm Bank residence by the respected architect and designer George Walton. I believe this very recipe book was used by Mrs Leetham in that residence, and possibly after its conversion to a hotel, the very same Elm Bank hotel that still stands on The Mount, close to York Racecourse.

Tragically, Sidney Leetham died at around the time the last recipe was added to this book (S. Leetham, August 1929), with a large chunk of empty pages remaining to be filled. His wife followed him within a year of his death (A. Leetham, April 1930).

It is difficult to source the full provenance of this book, in that it was not solely Mrs Leetham's duty to compile the recipes, as can be witnessed by the many hands involved, often with origin cited below the specific recipe. One can imagine cooks participating, encouraged by the wife of a prominent York resident, but not perhaps the multitude of other contributors, such as Goathland, Burnholme, Moorlyn, etc.

The most obvious difference within is the use of units now alien to us in contemporary times, such as the gill, or drachm. A list of modern conversions is available after the contents page.

Contents

Conversion Notes:

19th Century Units

1 Quart=1 quarter of a gallon/2 pints/4 cups
1 Gill= ¼ pint
2 pints= 1 quart
20 fluid oz= 1 pint
5 fluid 0z= 1 gill
10 fluid oz=1 cup
2 cups=1 pint
1lb= 16 oz

Conversion to metric:

1lb= 454 grams
½ lb= 227 grams
¼ lb= 113.5 grams
1 pint= 568 millilitres
½ pint= 284 millilitres
¼ pint= 142 millilitres
1 cup= 284 millilitres
1 gill= 142 millilitres
1 quart= 1.136 litres

Soups

Asparagus Soup

50 heads of asparagus, trim them and then throw into boiling water and boil 5 minutes. Keep the tops of 20 or so for a garnish. Bring 1 ½ pints of stock to a boil throw in the asparagus. Boil until quite soft ½ hour. Pass through a hair sieve, mix one desert spoon of arrowroot with a little cold water. Pour stock into it, season and return to pan, stir until it boils, add ½ pint of warmed cream and milk. And the asparagus tips boiled in salt and water and a little sugar and it is ready. N.b. the stock must be flavoured white stock.

White Stock: arrowroot, seasoning, cream, milk, salt, sugar

Bonne Femme Soup

¾ pint good white stock
¼ pint of cream
Yolk of an egg
2 tablespoons each of finely shredded lettuce, cucumber, spinach.
2 tablespoonfuls of young peas
½ oz of butter
½ teaspoonful castor sugar
Salt and pepper

Melt the butter in a pan, add the vegetables and sugar, toss in the butter, and then pour on the stock which must be boiling, season, let them simmer for 10 minutes. Beat up the egg and add the cream to it, pour the boiling stock on to it, and send to table at once. N.B. Do not allow the soup to boil after the eggs and cream are added.

Consommé aux Macaroni

Macaroni which must be thrown into boiling water. Boiled until tender. Add to soup last thing.

Consommé aux Quenelles

Clear soup garnished with very small quenelles poached and added last thing.

Consommé Jardinière

Tiny shreds of carrots cut from the outside and boiled, also turnips, peas, asparagus, herbs and shreds of lettuce and any thing cut small will do.

Consommé Julienne

Clear soup garnished with tiny shreds of carrot and turnip. Once cooked, cut the vegetables and throw into boiling water and salt for 12 minutes.

Consommé Royal

1 whole egg
1 yolk
2 tablespoons of cream
Salt and pepper
Seasoning

Beat the eggs, add cream and seasoning, well grease 2 cups, pour half the custard into one cup, colour the rest pink and pour into the other cup. Cover with greased paper and steam very slowly until quite firm, but not broken, let it get cold, cut into fancy shapes, first rinse in cold water and place carefully in the soup.

Friar Tuck Soup

1 quart clear soup
2 eggs

Boil up the soup but when in the act of boiling strain the eggs into it. They will instantly curdle and form a network in the soup. Let it boil a minute or two to cook them.

Game Soup
(Potage de Gibier)

3 pints of rather weak stock flavoured with vegetables
1 lb bones of game
1 oz of butter
¼ pint of sherry
Arrowroot

Make the stock hot, fry the pieces of game in the butter then put them into the stock and allow them to simmer gently for about 2 hours, then strain and to every pint of stock take half an oz of arrowroot and mixed with a little cold water, stir the hot stock into it, return to the pan and stir until it boils, season, add sherry, and if there are any nice pieces of the best meat cut up and put into the soup.

Gravy Soup

1 lb shin of beef
Salt and pepper to taste
A little celery
Parsley
Carrot
2 large onions fried brown
Rinse well with cold water, stir very slowly in a jar in the oven, only makes about a pint of soup.

Green Pea Soup

The white part of two or three Cos lettuces
2 cucumbers
2 sprigs of mint
3 onions
A little parsley
White pepper and salt

A full pint of young peas
5 oz of butter

Put these ingredients into a stew pan and let them stew gently in their own liquid for an hour. Boil another pint of peas till tender and pulp them through a colander and add to all a quart of beef stock.

Kidney Soup

Take 2 lb shin of beef
2 oz kidneys
Half a cupful of whole rice

Cover with water, add a little salt and skim carefully as it comes to the boil. Let it boil slowly for 2 hours, then take out the kidneys and let it boil 2 hours longer. Put it through a hair sieve and return to the pan. Have the kidneys cut and trimmed, add to the soup, boil for half an hour, and season with pepper and salt. An improvement: 1 carrot, 1 turnip, 1 onion, 1 celery.

Kidney Soup II

1 lb of shin of beef
4 pints cold water
1 ½ oz of butter
1 ox kidney
1 onion
1 carrot
½ a turnip
4 cloves and bouquet of herbs and salt
Tablespoonful and half of Cornflour
Sherry

Cut all fat from the meat and cut into small pieces. Place in a pan with the water and bring to a boil, skim and simmer gently for 2 hours. Slice the kidney and remove fat. Flour and fry in some of butter very quickly, make a nice brown, add to the soup. Clean, slice and fry vegetables in rest of the butter, add them with the herbs, cover and simmer for 3 hours longer, strain though a hair sieve and keep pieces of kidney until next day. Remove the fat from top of the stock, take a tablespoonful and a half of cornflour, mix and stir into the hot stock until it boils, add sherry to taste, browning and pieces of kidney cut into small pieces.

Kidney Soup III

1 lb ox kidney
1 small onion stuck with 4 cloves
The trimmings from a head of celery
1 small carrot and turnip

Stew the kidney very gently in just enough stock to cover it, for 8 hours, then pound in mortar and pass through a fine hair sieve. Mix with enough good stock to make it the consistency of good thick cream. Season well and just make it come to a boil and it will be ready to serve. 1 kidney enough for soup for 4 people.

Oxtail Soup

Take 2 lbs shin and 2 oxtails notched at the joints, and put them on in a pan, cover with water. Add ½ teacupful of whole rice and a little salt. Skim carefully as it comes to the boil, and let it boil slowly for two hours. Then take out the tails. Let it boil two hours longer taking care that it be not too much reduced. Strain through a hair sieve, skim and return to the pan. Cut the tails quite through where they have been notched, dividing the larger pieces, add to the stock, boil slowly for half an hour and season to taste.

Oxtail Soup II

1 oxtail
1 oz lean ham
1 carrot
1 onion
3 sticks celery
2 cloves
1 bunch of herbs

1 oz butter
Salt
1 oz cornflour
20 pepper corns
3 pints of stock
1 glass sherry
1 tablespoon mushroom ketchup

Cut the tail into joints, fry in butter, shred the vegetables, fry them, after tail is browned, put into the stock, with the salt and peppercorn, seasoning. Let it boil and stir well, let the whole simmer gently 4 hours, strain it and next day remove the fat and thicken with cornflour, boil till thickened before dishing up, add the wine and ketchup, and stir in a piece of butter the size of a nut.

Oyster Soup

Make some stock of veal and add 1 gill of cream and some oysters, but the cream and oysters must be put in a short time before being served. Thicken with arrowroot.

Oyster Soup II

½ pint of white stock, veal or mutton (boned meat will make it one)
2 pints of milk

Boil the stock and milk (gently) together with 3 black and 3 white peppercorns, 1 blade of mace tied in a piece of muslin for ½ an hour, take out the seasoning and add 2 spoonfuls of cornflour and the liquid from the oysters then simmer ¼ hour longer lay the oysters at the bottom of the tureen and pour the boiling soup over, add 1 gill of cream 10 oysters and the soup will do for 8 people.

Stock for Clear Soup

2 lbs shin of beef
1 lb knuckle of veal
¼ lb ham

3 quarts of cold water
2 onions
1 ½ oz of butter
1 carrot
½ turnip
2 pieces of celery
4 cloves
Bouquet of herbs
½ teaspoon of salt

Cut the beef, veal and ham into small pieces, place in a pan, add the cold water and bring to a boil, skim carefully and simmer for 2 hours. Slice and fry the onion in the butter, clear the rest of the vegetables, and add them with the onion to the rest of the stock, put in the cloves and herbs and simmer it for three hours longer, then strain through a hair sieve and it is ready to clear when the fat has been removed.

Tapioca Cream Soup

1 pint white stock
¼ pint cream
1 oz French tapioca
Yolk of 2 eggs
Pepper and salt

Boil the stock, season it, throw in the tapioca, simmer ten minutes or until the tapioca is clear. Beat the yolks of the eggs and add the cream to them. Pour the boiling stock upon it and then it is ready to serve. Cream and eggs are better put in the tureen.

To Clear Soup

Take all the fat from the top of the stock and place in a clean smooth pan. To every quart of stock take the whites of 3 eggs, whisk up stiffly and whisk into stock with the seasoning. If the stock is a jelly, just melt it before adding the eggs. bring to a boil, boil 5 minutes then strain through a clean towel kept for the purpose. The soup will take its name from the garnish, which should always be added cooked after clearing the soup.

To make the white soup

Take the fat off the above stock and bring it to a boil. To every quart of stock take about 2 tablespoonfuls of cornflour. Mix it with milk and pour the boiling stock on it and stir till it boils. Add to every quart of stock ½ pt cream or cream and milk mixed. Serve with fried or toasted bread.

Tomato Soup

1 quart of stock
2 oz of crushed tapioca or sago
2 oz lean ham (uncooked)
1 oz butter
1 small onion
1 carrot boiled in the stock

Melt the butter in the pan, put in the tomato, onion and ham. Let it simmer until tender. Have the stock boiling and throw in the tapioca. Pass the tomatoes through a hair sieve. Put all together and give it a boil. Add a little pepper and salt.

Tomato Soup II/ Tomato Cream

1 ½ pints of white stock
½ a tin of tomatoes
1 oz butter
2 tablespoons cornflour
½ pint cream
Salt, pepper and cochineal

Place tomatoes and butter in a pan and simmer 20 minutes. Boil the stock, mix cornflour with milk, pour boiling hot stock on to it, season, return to pan, stir till it boils and cools well, now pass tomatoes through a hair sieve or strained. Add this to the soup, add cream made warm and a few drops of cochineal to colour and the soup is ready.

Vegetable Soup

Cut carrots, turnips, celery and onion into very tiny squares. Fry for ¼ hour and then add pepper, salt and stock - boil till tender, then thicken and add a little milk.

White Stock

2 lbs knuckle of veal
½ lb ham
½ pt water
2 onions
2 pieces of celery
Some herbs
½ blade of mace
20 pepper corns
Herbs of parsley, thyme and bay leaf
1 teaspoonful of salt

Cut up the veal and ham and put into a pan of water: bring to the boil and skin. Simmer 2 hours and then add vegetables and flavouring and simmer for 2 hours longer and strain through a hair sieve. (keep the pan lid on).

White stock II

2 lb knuckle of veal
½ lb lean ham
5 pints cold water
2 onions
½ blade of mace
½ a teaspoonful salt
½ a turnip
2 pieces celery
A bouquet of herbs
20 pepper corns

4 inches lemon rind

**Recipes mentioned by title but without ingredients or cooking instructions were:

Chestnut Soup, Bisque of Oysters, Crab Soup, Lobster soup, Palestine Soup, Snack Turtle, Clear Oxtail Soup

Entrees Hot

Chicken Cutlets

3 oz cooked chicken
1 oz lean ham or tongue
1 oz butter
1 oz flour
¼ pint white stock
1 tablespoon cream
Salt, pepper, and cayenne

Melt the butter in a pan, then add the flour, the stock and seasoning, stir well and let it boil for a few minutes, then add the chicken and ham, which must be very finely minced, then the cream and a teaspoon of lemon juice, mix all well together and turn on to a plate to cool. When quite cold, shape into cutlets, dip each cutlet into well beaten egg and then in some breadcrumbs and fry in boiling fat, till they are a nice golden colour. Stick into each cutlet a small piece of macaroni to form the bone, dish up and fill in the centre with fried parsley.

Chicken Cutlets II

Add the prepared meat while the sauce is hot and mix with chicken stock instead of milk, adding about a tablespoon of cream after the mixture is cooked, which takes about 10 minutes. Spread the mixture on a plate and when cold shape into cutlets and fry in boiling fat in frying basket.

Crab Cutlets

Take 2 or 3 crabs, according to the size, pick and season with pepper, mace, cayenne and a little anchovy. Mix with an egg, dredge in as much flour as will make into a paste, make it into cakes, stew them with bread crumbs, fry them brown, serve with brown gravy.

Cutlets Provençal

1 pint of stock
1 carrot
1 turnip
1 onion

Let them come to the boil, then put in eight cutlets (see cutlets) and stew gently for 1 hour, then press the cutlets and when cold coat them with tomato sauce, then set once again with aspic jelly and dish on salad.

Tomato sauce for the above:

Melt 2 oz butter, fry 1 carrot, 1 turnip, 1 onion, 2 celery, 1 rasher of bacon. Brown them, add three bay leaves; parsley, cloves, peppercorns, 6 fresh tomatoes or ½ tin tomatoes. Let all simmer, reduce strain, and add ½ pint strong aspic jelly.

Dumplings

½ lb flour
3 oz finely chopped suet
¼ teaspoonful of salt
½ gill water

Chop the suet, mix well with flour. Add salt, make into a smooth paste with the water which you should add by degrees. Roll out and make into small round dumplings, 9 to 12.

Durham Cutlets

¼ lb of cold meat minced finely
1 oz butter
1 oz flour
½ pint stock
1 small onion boiled and minced finely
About a teaspoonful of chopped parsley
Salt and pepper

A pinch of cayenne

Melt the butter in a pan - add the flour to it. Stir these well together. Then add the stock. Stir until well boiled - add the meat seasoning to taste. Turn the mixture into a plate. Let it get cold. Make into the shape of small cutlets. Brush over with egg and bread crumb and fry in hot fat - to be drained on paper.

Fowl Kromeskies

Remains of cold fowl minced and mixed with cream, pepper and salt. Fold the mixture in thin slices of fat bacon. Then roll in very thin puff paste and dip in batter and fry in boiling lard.

Batter: ¾ cup flour, 1 egg white, 1 tablespoon oil and quarter pint warm water.

Kromeskies of Chicken

2 oz cooked chicken
½ oz butter
¾ oz flour
¼ pint of stock
1 tablespoon cream
Salt, pepper and cayenne
Very thin strips of bacon
Frying batter

Chop the chicken, melt the butter in a pan, add flour, and then the stock. Stir until they boil, cook well, put in the chicken, cream and seasoning, allow the mixture to cool. When cold, take a little of the mixture, place it on a very thin strip of bacon and roll the bacon round it, getting only one layer of bacon round it, dip in batter and fry in hot dripping.

Mutton Cutlets

2lbs of cud of neck of mutton

Saw off the chine bone and cut the rib bones short. Now divide into cutlets. Cut off the pieces of fat. Trim and season with a little pepper and salt. Dip into egg and then into bread crumbs and fry in hot dripping (do not cover with dripping). When browned on one side turn over and baste well. Small cutlets about 5 minutes to fry.

Potato border for cutlets.

1 lb steamed potatoes
1 oz butter
The yolk of 1 egg
Salt and pepper

Mash the potatoes - melt the butter and add to the potatoes with egg and seasoning. Make it into a long roll on a floured board - then place on a greased tin in the shape of a ring and brush with beaten egg and mask with knife or fork and brown quickly in the oven.

Quenelles of Rabbits, Veal or Chicken

Cut the meat from the back shoulders and legs of rabbit, pound well in a mortar, then rub through a hair sieve - put in a basin, add a little pepper, salt and stir to the right substance with cream. Grease the quenelle tins with butter, and first put in some finely chopped ham or tongue, then the mixture of rabbit. Put tissue paper over the tins, which put into a dripping tin, with a little water just covering the bottom of tin, Steamed in the oven for 10 minutes and dish up round a wall of potatoes and green vegetables in the centre.

Sausage Croquettes

1 lb sausage meat
1 beaten egg
½ lb cooked potatoes
Bread crumbs
A pinch dried thyme
Salt and pepper

Rub the potatoes through a sieve, season well and add the sausage meat and thyme. Make it into little rolls on a floured board. Brush them with beaten egg and roll them in breadcrumbs, then fry them in smoking dripping until well browned: drain them and serve on a dish paper and garnish with watercress. Slightly thickened brown gravy or tomato sauce may be sent to table separately to serve with them.

Savoury Semolina

1 cup semolina
1 pint milk
1 cup grated cheese
½ pint water
Pepper, salt

Sprinkle semolina into boiling water and milk. Simmer for 20 minutes. Add cheese and seasoning, put into a greased pie-dish. Put a few scraps of fat on top, brown in a good oven.

Veal Cutlets

Either a slice from a fillet of veal or the thin end of loin of veal, about 2 lbs, or 1 ½ lbs of fillet, a little salt, pepper and bread crumbs. Cut the veal into small pieces, about the size of a 5 shilling piece, season, then dip in beaten egg, then bread crumbs. Fry them in hot, clean dripping, arrange on a potato block, and put the cabbage puree round them. For the block, 1 lb steamed potatoes, 1 oz of butter, 1 egg, salt; mash the potatoes, add butter melted, yolk of egg and seasoning. Mix well together, make into a long block, like a roll of butter, brush over with beaten egg, then mark with a knife and fork. Brown potatoes in the oven quickly.

Zephyr of Pheasant (an entrée)

Any remains of pheasant may be used in this dish. Take 4 oz of the finest of the meat, pound it well in a mortar, with 2 tablespoonfuls of white stock. Press through a sieve, add to this the yolks of 2 eggs, a little nutmeg, pepper and salt. Now put into a basin ½ gill of cream, whisk until stiff, then add to the other ingredients, a little at a time, stirring it very gently all the time. Butter some small moulds, ornament them with truffles cut into dice, fill, them three parts full, cover with white paper. Put them in a stew pan with a little water.

**Recipes mentioned by title but without ingredients or cooking instructions were:

Grenadines, Fillets of Beef a la Soufflés, Cutlets a la Reform, Cutlets Braised, Veal Quenelles, Veal Fillets (larded), Sweetbreads a la Crème, Sweetbreads Fried, Sweetbreads au casise, sweetbread vol-au-vont, Crème de Volaille, Fricasee of Chicken, Chicken Quenelles, Cutlets a la Reine, Chicken Soufflé, Fillets of Beef a la Douglas, Stuffed Hare, Kidney a la Louisville, Lobster Soufflé, Little Cases of Chicken a la S Claire, Pigeons a la Grand Prix, Devilled Kidneys, Vol-au-vont Kidney

Entrees Cold

Dinner Buns

2 lbs flour
½ worth of yeast (I assume a "worth" is a 19th century sachet)
1 egg and a little butter worked in with the milk and butter warmed.
A pinch of salt.

**Recipes mentioned by title but without ingredients or cooking instructions were:

Quenelles a la Russe, Mutton Cutlets a la Provencale, Chaud Froid Chicken, Tomatoes a la Crème de Volaille, Chaux Froid of Pigeon a la Castilianne, Boned Chicken, Salantine Crème Pie

Hors d'oeuvres and Cold Savouries

Celery Cream

¼ pint of stiff whipped cream
1 tablespoon grated cheese
A pinch of salt and cayenne
3 tablespoons of shredded celery

Stir cheese, salt, pepper into the cream then add celery. Pile a teaspoonful of the mixture on a parmena or a plain milk biscuit. Makes 12 savouries.

Croutes a la Jambon

Fry some croutons till a nice golden brown about the size of a crown (old British coin), mash over with ham puree. Made as follows:

4 oz cooked ham
1 hard boiled egg pounded till smooth, dust of cayenne. Pass through a sieve and pile on croutes, decorate with whipped cream if liked and parsley. Eggs left from breakfast and scraps of ham can be used.

Rissoles in Paste

½ oz butter
½ oz flour
1/8 of pint of good stock
2 oz beef or mutton
¼ a small onion (scalded)
Salt and pepper
Egg and bread crumbs
Short or flaky crust

Chop the meat and onion finely, melt butter in a pan, add the flour and then the stock. Stir until it boils, cook well, add meat and onions, season and allow it to get cold. Roll out a piece of good pastry very thinly. Place small pieces at even distances and fold the paste over, wetting it first, cut out with a round cutter, dip in beaten egg and then in bread crumbs and fry in hot dripping. Short paste: 2 oz flour, 1 oz butter, very little cold water.

Savoury Christina

Some pieces of bread cut into kite shapes and fried a golden brown.

2 oz butter
Yolks of 3 hard boiled eggs
½ teaspoon of anchovy paste
Salt, pepper, cayenne and a few drops of carmine

Pound the yolks of the eggs with the anchovy paste, work the butter to a cream and add that to the eggs. Season and colour slightly with carmine, pass through a hair sieve, spread the pieces of fried bread. With a little anchovy paste, pass the butter through a forcer on to the broad end of the bread. Decorate the other end with the remaining yolk of egg, that has been passed through a wire sieve and garnish with green butter or whipped cream, according to taste.

**Recipes mentioned by title but without ingredients or cooking instructions were:

Croutes a la Grand Hotel, Croutes a la Francaise, Anchovy Salad, Celery Cream, Anchovy Croutes, Sardine Croutes, Lax sur croutes, Anchovy Rissoles, Chaux au Fromage, Anchovy Baskets, Croutes a la St Stephen

Hot Savouries

Croustades a la Victoria

3 oz flour
1 ½ oz butter
½ an egg
Salt, pepper and cayenne

Rub the butter into the flour and mix the seasoning with the egg and a little water and make into a very stiff paste. Roll out very thin and line some small deep patty tins. Prick the bottoms with a fork, then line them with a paper well greased, on the pastry side and fill them up with new rice. Bake in a fairly quick oven and when they are cooked, take out the rice and if the pastry is not quite done, return them to the oven for a few minutes longer. Then place in each croustade a small piece of dried haddock, which has been cooked in milk, then pour over a cheese cream. Put them into a very hot oven, just to brown the cheese.

Ham Croutons

Make some rounds of hot toast and put a little buttered egg on each - then sprinkle some finely chopped ham on the egg. Serve very hot.

Macaroni Pudding

½ lb cold minced meat
2 oz bread crumbs
2 oz cooked rice or macaroni
1 egg beaten
1 teacupful stock mixed with ½ oz flour, flavouring, salt, pepper, tomatoes, onion sauce or 1 spoonful of anchovy essence.

Grease a cake tin or basin - coat it with bread crumbs and pack in the mixture. It should first come to the top of the tin. Put more crumbs and a sheet of buttered paper over, then bake in a moderate oven for an hour. It should turn out brown and firm. Pour gravy around it or steam for an hour and a half.

Yorkshire Pudding

6 oz flour
2 eggs whole
½ cup cold water

Add milk to thickness of double cream for Yorkshire pudding

**Recipes mentioned by title but without ingredients or cooking instructions were:

Profiterole de Parmesan, Croutes aux Champignons, Croutes a la Jubilee, Anchovy Éclairs, Foi de Volatile a la Diable, Lax Sur Croutes

Meat Dishes

Braised Steak

1 lb beef steak
2 oz bread crumbs and fat bacon, salt, pepper, herbs, an egg, a teaspoonful of anchovy essence and a tablespoonful or two of gravy with a little glaze or gelatine dissolved in it.

Mince the meat finely and mix the rest with it, except the white of an egg. Shape it into a roll, coat with white of an egg, then cover it with more crumbs shaking off loose ones. Turn it about in hot fat until it is a golden brown: drain away the fat and pour in sufficient stock to half cover your roll: cook gently for an hour and a half, turn over during the cooking and just before serving add a little red currant jelly to your gravy. It should be thickened with browned flour.

Kidneys Maitre d' Hotel

Skin the kidneys and split lengthwise, take out the core and put in skewers. Let a piece of butter the size of a nut (for 2 or 3 kidneys) melt in the frying pan and lay in the kidneys. Fry fairly quickly for 7 or 8 minutes, taste all the time. 1 oz of butter (for 2 or 3 kidneys), beat to a cream, add 1 teaspoon lemon juice and lastly chopped parsley. Put kidneys on hot toast and the butter on the kidney at the last moment.

Potted Beef

1 lb lean beef. Cut up in squares.

Put in a stew jar in the oven. Just cover with cold water and let it reduce in the oven, so as to get all the juice into the meat. when it comes to a boil, put in a little salt and pepper, stew gently until tender, 1 ½ to 2 hours, then pass 6 times through a mincer, beat well, add liquid by degrees, season to taste, then put in a little oiled butter, heat again, press well into pots and cover with butter.

Sausage Fritters

½ lb sausages made up to the size of a halfpenny - then dried in flour and dipped into thick batter and dropped into very hot fat. Some fresh dry parsley can be thrown into the fat for a few seconds only and served with the fritters - or equal quantities of liver and bacon (fat) rubbed through a wire sieve - till it forms a pulp seasoned with herbaceous mixture.

Savoury Roll

Mix all equal weight of mashed potatoes and cold meat (minced) - a little ham or bacon if you have it - to 1 lb meat add 2 well beaten eggs. 1 oz butter (dissolved) with seasoning to taste. 1 spoonful chopped parsley and a little thick gravy. Shape it like a roll pudding and brown it in a quick oven. Reserve a little egg for brushing over the top and you can put a few heaps of mixed pickles here and there, heating them first in a little gravy.

Poultry and Game

Cassolettes of Chicken

Prepare some nice mashed potatoes and mix with them the yolk of one egg, a little cream and nicely season with salt and pepper. Roll out on to a floured board and with a plain round cutter, cut them out about the same size, as for a meat patty. Brush them over with beaten egg and roll them in bread crumbs. This must be done twice and then with a smaller cutter, make a ring round the top, fry them in very hot fat, till they are a nice golden colour. When they are done, drain them on a wire sieve and with a small knife, take off the lid, that has been marked with the small cutter and with the handle of a spoon, take out all the soft part of the potato, leaving the cassolette quite dry and firm. Fill each one with some nicely minced and seasoned chicken and ham, or game when in season. Put on the lid of each and garnish with parsley.

Chicken Aspic

Stew a chicken in well flavoured stock. When cold remove the white flesh, pound it in a mortar, pass it through a sieve, then mix it with one egg, the yolks of three and a little cream. Flavour with nutmeg, pepper and salt. Take a plain round mould, pour into it a layer of aspic, then a layer of the mixture and so on till the mould is full, when quite firm, turn out and garnish with chopped aspic jelly and small heaps of chives and tarragon.

Chicken Bouchees

¼ lb cooked chicken
1 oz ham or tongue
1 oz butter
¼ pint milk and cream mixed
Short pastry
Chopped parsley
¼ pint stock from chicken bones - flavour with onion, mace, lemon rind and pepper corns

Salt, pepper and cayenne

Line some small moulds with pastry (see pastry): prick the bottoms - line with greased paper and fill with rice and bake in a moderate oven. Chop the chicken and ham finely. Melt butter in a pan, add the flour, then the stock gradually. Stir till boiling, add milk and cream and seasonings and chopped meat and fill the pastry cases. Whip the whites of eggs to a stiff froth, pile them on top - sprinkle with chopped ham on tongue and parsley and set in a moderate oven to dry.

Chicken Cream

Take 3 oz of the breast of a cold chicken
½ teaspoonful of mayonnaise sauce
One tablespoonful of white sauce
3 tablespoonfuls of aspic jelly
Salt and pepper and cayenne

Chop and pound the chicken and add the other ingredients.

Chicken in Casserole

2 oz butter
1 onion fried in the butter
The chicken cut into 10 pieces
2 lbs tomatoes, cut and added.
Also pepper and salt (a few pepper corns)

Add 1 pint of water - and simmer 1 hour very slowly. Add 8 potatoes, a few onions and simmer an hour more. Then thicken the gravy with a little flour.

Chicken Soufflé on Cheese

1 oz butter
1 ½ oz flour
½ pint milk

2 eggs
Pepper and salt
2 chicken legs

Melt the butter and flour in the pan together then add the milk and stir until it thickens. Cook well for a minute or two, take off the fire and allow to cool. Then add the pepper and salt and the yolks of eggs, stir well, then put in the chicken minced very fine (or 1 ½ oz of cheese for a cheese soufflé) (and the well beaten whites which must be a stiff froth). Stir these in gently, and put into a buttered soufflé case, with a paper band round the outside, the top part must be greased. Bake or steam 40 minutes.

Compote of Pigeon

3 pigeons
1 pint brown stock well flavoured
1 onion
4 cloves
½ blade of mace
1 tablespoon flour
Salt and pepper
A little warm glaze
Mashed potatoes
Cooked vegetables (any)

Draw and clean the pigeon and cut into four pieces. Put into a pan with the stock and flavouring, bring to a boil and let it simmer until tender. Now thicken the gravy with flour, take out the pigeons and brush over with glaze. Dish up on a border of mashed potatoes just cooked. Lay in centre and strain the gravy round.

Vol-au-vent of Chicken

6 oz chicken
2 oz lean ham or tongue
1 ½ oz butter
½ pint white stock
¼ pint milk and cream mixed

The grated rind of a small ½ lemon
Salt, pepper and cayenne

Cut the chicken and ham into small square pieces, melt the butter in a pan, add the flour and cook for about 3 minutes. Then add the stock and milk slowly. Add the seasoning and boil for about 3 minutes. Add the cut up chicken and tongue and it is then ready for use.

Puff pastry for vol-au-vent

½ lb flour
½ lb butter
A little cold water
2 teaspoons of lemon juice

Rub 2 oz of the butter into the flour, then mix into a stiff paste with the lemon juice and water. Roll, cut and place the rest of the butter on it, fold and roll out again. Fold in 3 each time and roll it out 7 times altogether, allowing ½ an hour between each time of rolling. It must be kept in a very cool place and must be cut out with a vol-au-vent cutter in three pieces. Leave the bottom piece whole, but cut out the centre of the other two pieces, with a smaller cutter each piece should be cut ½ inch thick.

Fish and Shellfish

Bombay Toast

Take 1 oz of anchovies, wash, bone and pound them in a mortar, with 1 oz of fresh butter, till reduced to a smooth paste. Melt the anchovy butter in a saucepan and as it melts add the yolks of 2 eggs. Stir till the consistency of cream, add cayenne to taste. Spread the mixture on slices of bread, fried brown and serve very hot.

Crab Soufflés

2 oz butter
2 oz flour
½ pint thin cream
6 anchovies
3 eggs
1 large crab
Pepper and cayenne

Melt the butter in a pan, add flour, then cream gradually, stir till boiling and cook well - add the anchovies (boned and rubbed through a sieve), seasoning, the meal from the crab, then yolks of eggs and lastly the whites whipped very stiff - pour the mixture into some well buttered soufflé cases round which a band of paper has been fastened and bake in a quick oven for 15 minutes. Serve quickly.

Croute a la Jubilee

Take half a good sized dried haddock and remove all the bones and skin and rub the flesh through a wire sieve. Fry some croutons, which should be a ¼ of an inch thick and 2 inches in diameter and quite crisp.

Mix with the haddock enough warm butter to make it moist and season it with a little cayenne pepper. With a hot knife spread a layer on a crouton, place a bearded oyster, also flavoured with cayenne, in the middle and entirely cover it with more haddock, making the shape pyramidal and the outside smooth. Place on a tin, cover them with a buttered paper and just before putting them in the oven, pour a little warm butter over them. Cook them in a moderately hot oven for 5 or 6 minutes, sprinkle with lobster spawn over them and a sprig of parsley in the centre.

Fish a la Volles-cke

Take the cold remains of boiled fish and break into small pieces. Make some good white sauce with cornflour. Grate in some cheese, pepper and salt to taste, then add the fish. Pour into a well buttered pie dish or shells. Grate cheese on the top and some small pieces of butter. Place in oven till a nice golden brown.

Fish Soufflé

½ lb fish
3 eggs
2 oz flour
1 gill fish stock
1 oz butter
1 gill cream

Put butter and flour into a saucepan, mix well over the fire, add stock and stir until it thickens, when cooked put the panada (via google: butter, flour, and fish stock or milk represent the panada) and fish into a mortar and pound them well together, adding eggs one at a time also salt and a little cayenne pepper. Put mixture through a sieve, stir whipped cream lightly in, well butter a mould, pour in mixture, cover with buttered paper and steam gently ½ an hour, turn out and pour white sauce over and serve very hot.

Lobster Cornets

1 oz butter
1 oz flour
4 oz lobster

¼ pint of milk
A little salt, pepper, cayenne
A little lemon juice

Melt the butter in a pan. Stir in the flour until smoothly mixed. Then add the milk. Stir until it comes to the boil and let it cool 2 or 3 minutes. Then add the seasoning and lemon juice, and lobster finely chopped - add to the mixture. Fill the cornets and place in each a sprig of parsley.

Lobster Mixture

1 lobster (1/6)
1 oz butter
1 oz flour
¼ pint white stock
¼ pint cream and milk mixed
Salt, pepper, cayenne and about one tablespoonful of hot spawn.

Take the meat from the lobster and chop it slightly. Wash the shell and let it simmer in the stock 10 minutes. Melt the butter in a pan - add the flour, the strained stock milk and cream and the lobster spawn pounded and passed through a sieve. Stir it until it boils, then add the lobster meat and seasoning.

Offreurs Toast

1 oz butter
Yolk of an egg
1 teaspoonful anchovy sauce
½ teaspoon of Worcester Sauce
¼ pint of milk
8 drops of lemon juice

Put milk into a pan , thicken with a little cornflour. When cooled stir in the yolk of egg and other ingredients. Skin and bone as many sardines as required. Put them gently into the hot mixture, allow to get thoroughly hot. Dish up on strips of toast or fried croutons.

Oyster Patty Mixture

½ score of oysters
¾ oz butter
¾ oz flour
¼ pint oyster liquor and stock mixed
2 or 3 tablespoons cream
Salt, pepper, cayenne and lemon juice

Beard the oysters, melt the butter in a pan. Add the flour and cook them a few minutes, then add the stock. Stir until it boils. Now add the cream and teaspoonfuls of oysters. Just make hot and full the patty cases with the mixture.

Rissoles aux Huitres

6 oz cooked veal
2 oz cooked ham
1 oz butter
1 oz flour
1 quart stock
1 teaspoonful essence of anchovy
1 teaspoonful Worcester sauce, salt and oysters, pepper and cayenne

Chop the veal and ham finely. Melt the butter, and add the flour, then the stock slowly and the sauces and seasoning. Bring to a boil and cook well. Add meat and allow to get cold. Divide the mixture into 8 pieces. Put a bearded oyster on each. Dip in egg and then bread crumbs and fry in hot fat, warm well and serve very hot.

Scalloped Oysters

Some well buttered scallop shells
1 oz butter
1 oz flour
¼ pint milk and oyster liquor mixed
A little lemon juice
Pepper and cayenne

Melt the butter in a pan and cook for a few minutes, but do not allow it to brown. Add the milk gradually, cook well and then add the oysters, pepper, cayenne and lemon juice. Put into scallop shells, cover with brown crumbs. Place in the oven for about 10 minutes and serve very hot, garnished with parsley. Allow 3 oysters for each shell.

Siberian Crab Jelly

Take off the stalks. Weigh the crabs. To each 1 ½ lbs of crabs add 1 pint of cold water, and boil gently till broken, but not to a pulp. Strain through a fine sieve. Weigh the juice and boil quickly for 10 minutes. Take it from the fire, stir in until dissolved 10 oz of preserving sugar to each 1 lbs of the juice weighed. Boil for 1 hour after it boils or till it sets.

**Recipes mentioned by title but without ingredients or cooking instructions were:

Ribbon Fillets of Sole, Fried Sole, Sole a la Colbert, Sole aux Crevettes, Sole a la Maitre d' Hotel, Sole au fin Blanc, Sole aux Gratin, Sole a la Parisienne, Oyster Cutlets, Lobster Cutlets, Scalloped Oysters, Devilled Haddock, Salmon Grilled Cutlets

Vegetable Dishes

Beetroot Hot

Fry a good sized Spanish onion till brown, then sprinkle about a desert spoon of flour into a pan and add a teaspoonful of sugar, tablespoonful of vinegar, a little pepper and salt and water to make it the consistency of cream. Stir the cooked beetroot in and when hot dish up with mashed potatoes round a ring.

Cauliflower Soufflé a la Baronne

Trim a nice cauliflower, put it to blanch, then rinse it and put it into boiling water with a little salt and let it cook till tender. Drain and cut it in neat pieces and place in a buttered soufflé dish with alternate layers of sliced tomatoes. Season with a very little salt and coralline pepper and fill the dish with a soufflé mixture and sprinkle over with a few browned breadcrumbs and place a few pieces of butter here and there on top. Bake in a moderate oven for 30 minutes. Dish up on a paper with napkin round and sprinkle with a little chopped parsley.

Mixture for sauce:

Mix 2 oz of butter
1 ½ oz flour
1 raw egg
Tiny dust of coralline pepper
A salt spoon of salt with not quite half a pint of cold milk.

Stir over the fire till it boils, then add 3 oz grated parmesan cheese and the whites of 1 egg that have been whipped stiff, with a pinch of salt.

Curried Lentils

¼ lb lentils well soaked and washed
½ pint of curry sauce (see Curry Sauce)

4 oz boiled rice

Simmer the lentils in the sauce for 2 hours. They must cook very slowly. Serve in a border of rice. Garnish with lemon and parsley.

Fried parsley

Pick and mash the parsley, dry in a cloth and fry till crisp and green, only fresh picked parsley will keep green.

German Salad

Cut up cold potatoes with an equal quantity of cooked beetroot. Put into a salad bowl with a teaspoonful of minced onion, a few pieces of celery cut in neat pieces, then pour over the following mixture:

½ teacupful of water
Small teacup of vinegar
2 tablespoons salad oil
1 tablespoon soft sugar
1 teaspoon salt and a little pepper

Allow to stand an hour before sending to table.

Mushrooms

Peel about a pint of button mushrooms, and throw into water with lemon juice as you do them. Put into a pan 1 oz butter, a squeeze of lemon, a little salt and pepper then add the mushrooms, cover pan with a lid and cook five minutes, strain and put a little stock to the gravy, thicken with flour a little, let the gravy first boil and pour over the mushrooms.

Potato Balls

1 lb mashed potatoes
1 egg

1 oz butter
Salt and pepper
Parsley chopped

Melt the butter, mix with the potatoes, salt, pepper, and a little of the egg beaten, flour the hands and form into balls, brush over with beaten egg. Roll in the crumbs and fry in smoking-hot fat until nicely browned. Drain and serve on a lace paper, be very careful not to over fry them, or they spoil.

Potato Surprises

2 oz minced meat
A little lemon rind
Seasoning
A little white sauce
Dried herbs

From the ingredients into balls. Put 1lb mashed potatoes in a basin, add ½ oz melted dripping, enough egg to bind or a little milk. Cover the balls with the potatoes. Fry in hot fat. Garnish with parsley.

Potted Beans and Lentils

½ pint washed beans or lentils
1 small onion
1 pint water
2 oz of fat
2 oz grated cheese
Salt and pepper to taste

Cosh the beans and onion until soft. Remove onion and strain beans. Rub through sieve, add fat etc. mix very well. Put into pots. Pour over a little margarine - use as potted mash and for sandwiches.

Red Cabbage

Wash the cabbage well, cut it very fine. Put a piece of fresh butter about the size of a walnut into the copper pan and then the cabbage. Add a tumbler of cold water and the necessary salt and let it gently simmer for one hour. Quarter of an hour before dishing it up, put two cooking apples into the pan to flavour it.

Short pastry

¼ lb flour
2 oz butter
Yolk of 1 egg
3 tablespoons Water

Rub butter into flour and mix with yolk and water to stiff paste.

Soufflé Potatoes

Take as many potatoes as are required, choose large ones, bake them well. Cut in half and scoop out the inside, pass the potatoes through a sieve, add a little pepper, salt, butter and a little milk, then fill the potato cases with the mashed potatoes and return to the oven to brown.

Stuffed Tomatoes

4 tomatoes
4 small rounds of toast
½ lb raw ham
1 teaspoonful of milk
1 oz bread crumbs
A little of the pulp of fruit

Put the ham into boiling water and let it cook for about 7 minutes, then chop it finely. Cut a small hole in the bottom of the tomatoes and take out some of the pulp. Lay the tomatoes downwards on a plate to drain. Mix the breadcrumbs, ham and a little of the pulp together, add seasoning and rind with the milk. Return the whole to the inside of the tomato and press well down. Put on a plate, cover with a greased paper and put in the oven for a few minutes to warm.

Melt some butter and with it brush round the edges of toast and roll them in the chopped parsley, until they are will coated round. Put the tomatoes in the middle of each round and a sprig of parsley in the centre of the tomato.

Tomato Salad

6 firm tomatoes
A little eschalot
A teaspoonful chopped parsley
Pepper, salt, a little vinegar
Salad oil

Dip the tomatoes in boiling water. Remove the skin, slice them in small quarters, grate the eschalot and chop very, very fine. Mix all the things together, sprinkling with vinegar, salad oil and a little castor sugar. Serve with roast meat.

Tomatoes

6 or 8 small tomatoes
Chicken cream
Aspic jelly
Truffles and a little parsley

Dip the tomatoes in boiling water for a second, cut a hole in the top and scoop out the inside. Fill with chicken cream, put the lid on again and decorate with small pieces of chicken and truffles, pour aspic jelly over it. When it is just setting, decorate the top with small pieces of parsley. Arrange them in a border mould with lettuce and aspic jelly.

Tomatoes Cheese

4 tomatoes chopped fine
An equal quantity of cheese cut into small pieces

Mix together with a little cream, season with salt and pepper (cayenne). Stir the mixture over the fire till it is dissolved. Have ready some slices of hot buttered toast. Pour on the mixture and serve up quickly.

Tomatoes Savoury

Rub 3 tomatoes through a sieve. Put pulp into a pan with a bit of butter and pinch of castor sugar, pepper and salt to taste. Cook for 5 minutes. Take off stove till nearly cold then add 2 well beaten eggs. Stir till mixture thickens, pour onto buttered toast. Serves 4 persons.

Vegetable Pie

¼ lb cooked carrot
¼ lb cooked turnip
¼ lb cooked onion
¼ lb cooked haricot beans
2 oz cooked lentils
2 lbs cooked potatoes
½ lb cooked rice or barley
2 or 3 tomatoes
1 oz margarine or dripping
1 ½ oz fine oatmeal browned in the oven
1 pint water, stock or barley water
Seasoning

Slice tomatoes, cook in margarine, remove them, add oatmeal and water to make a sauce. Season. Mash potatoes, grease a pie dish, line with potatoes. Put layers of the vegetable and sauce. Bake until very hot through.

Vegetarian Sausages

4 tablespoonfuls fried onion
6 tablespoonfuls bread crumbs
4 tablespoonfuls mashed potatoes or cooked rice
2 tablespoonfuls tomato pulp
2 tablespoonfuls fat,

A little sage and parsley
1 egg
Salt and pepper

Mix very well. Form into little rolls. Flour each. Fry or bake until brown.

**Recipes mentioned by title but without ingredients or cooking instructions were:

Artichokes Velleson, Artichokes Scalloped, Petit Crème de Pois, Petit Crème d' Asperges, Celery Villeroi, Puree of Spinach aux Oeufs, Tomatoes au gratin, Tomatoes Aux Mayonaise, Stuffed Cucumber, Brussel Sprouts and Parmesan, Cauliflower au gratin

Rice Dishes

Rice Cakes

½ lb flour
½ lb caster sugar
¼ lb ground rice
¼ lb butter
4 eggs
Currants
1 teaspoonful baking powder

Rice Cakes II

3 eggs
3 oz butter (melted)
3 oz rice
4 oz flour
6 oz sugar
1 teaspoonful baking powder

Rice Cakes III

½ lb sugar
3 oz butter
¼ lb flour
¼ lb ground rice
4 eggs
½ teaspoonful of baking powder
Flavour with lemon rind

Cream the butter, add sugar, then rice and flour, then eggs and baking powder. Bake in a quick oven till a light brown.

Spanish Rice

1 teacup of rice

5 tomatoes
3 small sweet peppers (cut up)
1 tablespoon of butter
1 tablespoon of sugar
1 pint of water

Mix and put in a stew pan (stir to prevent burning), a little salt and one onion. Cook an hour and serve as a vegetable.

Cheese and Egg Dishes

Baked Eggs

Boil 2 eggs hard, shell them, cut in halves lengthwise. Take out the yolk and mash up with a tablespoonful of bread crumbs, 2 tablespoons, milk, pepper and salt to taste, 1 oz of butter. Put mixture back into the whites. Next butter a gratin dish, spread bread crumbs. Stand eggs in and cover quickly with grated cheese and sprinkle over with browned bread, crumbs, a few bits of butter. Put into the oven until thoroughly hot and leave in the dish. If left in the oven too long, the eggs will be tough.

Cheese Biscuits and Cream

Make some cheese biscuits the usual way, only cut 3 different sizes. Put some cream mixed with parmesan cheese and cayenne pepper, slightly whipped, between each. Put one for the bacon and then a smaller one and a smaller one still on the top.

Cheese cream

4 oz gruyere cheese
3 tablespoons cream
Salt, pepper and cayenne

Put the cheese, cream and seasoning into a pan on the fire and stir till the cheese is melted. It should be like good thick cream, when poured on to the haddock.

Cheese Croquettes

1 oz butter
1 ½ oz flour
1 ½ oz grated parmesan cheese
¼ pint water
2 eggs, leaving out one white

Salt, pepper and cayenne

Melt the butter in a pan, add flour and then the water. Stir until they boil, cook well, put in the cheese and beaten egg, a little at a time, and season. Drop by teaspoons on hot fat and fry a nice brown. Serve hot at once.

Cheese Custard

2 or 3 oz of cheese in shavings, beaten up with 1 large or 2 small eggs, and about a ¼ pint of milk. Butter a dish well and bake a few minutes with a little butter on the top.

Cheese Eggs

2 eggs
3 oz grated cheese
4 tablespoons milk
½ oz butter
Salt, pepper and cayenne
2 or 3 slices buttered toast

Beat the eggs well, add cheese, milk and seasoning. Melt butter in a pan, add mixture or stir over a gentle heat till quite thick, then pile on rounds of toast and serve very hot garnished with parsley.

Cheese Ramekins

3 oz grated cheese
2 oz bread crumbs
1 oz butter
½ pint of milk
2 eggs
Salt and cayenne

Boil the milk, pour on the crumbs, add butter. When cool add yolks, cheese and seasoning. Whisk whites to stiff froth, stir lightly into the mixture. Fill cases 3 parts full and bake in a moderate oven 15 minutes, send to table quickly.

Cheese Soufflé or Fondue

½ oz butter
2 eggs
½ oz flour
1 ½ oz grated cheese
¼ pint milk or rather more
Salt, pepper, cayenne

Melt the butter in a pan, add the flour, then the milk. Stir until they boil, now allow to cool. Add the cheese, yolks of egg and seasoning. Whisk the whites to a stiff froth, stir them lightly into the mixture. Have ready a soufflé tin greased with butter and a band of greased paper tied round it. Pour in the mixture and bake in a quick oven for 20 minutes. Now put a paper frill round the tin or basin or a folded napkin and it is ready.

Cheese Soufflé (small)

Melt ½ oz of fresh butter in a saucepan, stir into it a tablespoonful of flour. When the two are well mixed, put in a small quantity of milk, 3 oz of parmesan cheese. Stir the mixture on a slow fire, till it assumes the appearance of thick cream. It must not boil. Then add some white pepper and if required a little salt. Keep stirring at a moderate heat for 10 minutes. Take the saucepan off the fire, stir the contents until quite cold. Then stir into that the yolks of 3 eggs beaten with a little milk and lastly the whites of 5 eggs whisked to a stiff froth. Half fill some small paper cases. Put them in the oven and bake from 10 to 15 minutes.

Cheese Straws

2 oz cheese
2 oz butter
2 oz flour

After carefully kneading together add the yolk of an egg, pepper and salt. Roll into a paste. Cut into straws and bake in a quick oven.

Eggs au Gratin

For the sauce:

1 oz butter
1 large tablespoonful flour
¼ pint milk
2 oz grated cheese

Grease as many scallop slices or small au gratin disks as eggs required. Break one egg in each dish. Pour the sauce over it. Bake 5 minutes for soft baked eggs.

Eggs Stuffed with Mushrooms

Boil hard, as many eggs as you require. When cold cut lengthwise, take out the yolks, pass through a sieve, season with a little pepper, salt, cayenne and cream. Chop fine a nice large mushroom. Fry in a little butter, mix with the yolk of eggs, put back into the halves. Dish up with cress or shred lettuce.

Macaroni Cheese

Boil the macaroni until quite tender, drain and put back into the pan. Have ready:

3 oz grated cheese
A few bread crumbs
½ a teaspoonful dry mustard
Pepper and salt to taste
½ a gill of milk

Stir well together over the fire, until a creamy mixture. Pour into a shallow dish. Scatter over a very few bread crumbs and small pieces of butter, and brown with a salamander (a type of broiler). Serve very hot.

Roulettes a la Pompeii

¾ lb puff pastry
1 oz flour
2 yolks of eggs
2 oz parmesan cheese
¼ pint cream
Not quite ½ pint milk
3 tablespoons white sauce
¼ oz gelatine
Small tablespoon grated horseradish
Cayenne and salt

Roll out the paste thinly. Stamp into rounds with a four inch cutter and fold round small roll tins. Fasten the join with egg or water, place on a baking tin, brush with beaten egg and bake in a quick oven till brown, then remove this. Mix the flour with a little cream, boil the milk and stir onto flour. Add the cheese, return to pan and stir till well cooked. Add the yolks and seasonings and when cool add the rest of cream whipped stiffly and fill the cases with the mixture. Dissolve the gelatine in a little milk. Add the horse radish and white sauce. Any remains of custard maybe added also. Strain it and when setting garnish the cases with the mixture passed through a fancy tube. Serve cold as an after dinner savoury or for supper.

Savoury (what they really mean by this is unsure)

Make some cases of the same kind of pastry as that used for cheese straws. Make a custard with the yolks of 2 eggs - a little milk - and 1 oz grated cheese - when cold pour into the cases and sprinkle a little grated cheese on the top. Serve when cold.

Scotch Eggs

Hard boiled eggs, covered with sausage meal (cut in half), dipped in egg and bread crumbs and fried and tomato sauce round.

Sandwiches

Cheese Sandwiches

Butter small slices of bread and make into sandwiches with thin slices of cheese. Dip in lightly beaten egg yolk to which has been added a little milk and salt. Fry the sandwiches brown in butter. Turn carefully so as not to separate.

Sandwich a la Wyndham

Hard boiled eggs, and anchovy butter and some green butter, put on slices of bread, cut through, to show the different colours.

Savoury mixture for sandwiches

To every 6 sardines 1 boned anchovy
20 capers in a pot of butter

Pound well and make into sandwich with either brown or white bread and butter, or spread on biscuits as a savoury.

Deserts and Puddings

A Delicious Pudding

1 tablespoonful flour
4 oz candied peel
3 oz beef suet chopped fine
4 oz bread crumbs
2 oz apricot jam
1 dessertspoonful of milk
3 eggs
Flavour with a teaspoon brandy
Beat eggs with the milk and mix well with the other ingredients.
Pour into a butter mould and steam 3 hours.

Apple Snow

½ pint of good custard
3 sponge cakes
6 oz roast apple pulp
6 oz castor sugar
Whites of 2 eggs
Juice of ½ a lemon

Cut up the sponge cakes in slices and lay them in a deep glass dish,
pour the custard when cool, over them. Add the sugar to the apple,
strain the lemon juice on it. Whisk up the whites of egg quite stiff,
whisk into the apple until it looks quite white like snow. Put on the
top of the soaked cakes and it is ready.

Apple Soufflé

Pare and cut the apples into quarters, stir until soft with sugar to
taste. Add a little butter and the yolks of 2 eggs. Whisk the whites
and pile on the top and bake.

Apricot Mould

Soak a teaspoonful of gelatine. Take two halves of apricot; crush them to pulp with a spoon. Mix with them ¾ cupful of cream or milk. Add sugar to taste. Dissolve the gelatine, mix it when cool with the apricot and mould when cold. Good for apple mould also.

Baked Batter Pudding

3 or 4 tablespoons of flour
A little salt
2 eggs dropped into the flour one at a time and beaten
½ pint of nice hot milk not boiled

Put into a buttered pie dish and bake or a mould and steam.

Baroness Pudding

½ lb flour
½ lb suet
½ lb raisins (stoned)
Small salt spoonful of salt.

Mix stiff with milk and boil 2 ½ hours in a cloth.

Bavarois a la Baronne

A little clear lemon jelly
½ oz blanched and finely shred pistachio nuts
1 oz of blanched and finely chopped sweet almonds
½ tin of apricots
½ pint of good custard
½ pint of cream
¾ oz gelatine dissolved in milk or water
About ½ teacup of water to dissolve gelatine

Line a mould with jelly, stir about 2 or 3 tablespoonfuls of the jelly into the almonds and nuts separately. When rather cool decorate the mould with pistachios and almonds and very small quarters of apricots, which have had a dab of carmine on one end. Add the custard to the cream, which must be whisked firm. Put in the rest of the apricots, about ¼ pint passed through a wire sieve. Add the gelatine dissolved in water. When beginning to set, turn into the line mould.

Blanc Mange

Soak 1 oz gelatine in a pint of new milk for 2 or 3 hours. Boil 2 or 3 laurel or bay leaves in 1 pint of milk. When boiling, pour over the soaked gelatine, stir till it dissolves. Add 4 or 5 oz of lump sugar. Strain through a muslin, stir occasionally till it thickens, and then pour into moulds.

Boiled Sponge and Apple Pudding

Some good cooking apples
3 oz flour
2 oz butter
2 oz sugar
1 egg
1 teaspoon baking powder

Rub butter in flour, add sugar and baking powder and mix with egg well beaten. Roll out the paste and line a plain mould with it. Fill with sliced apples, sweet meal, flavoured with a little lemon peel. Cover over with the paste and steam for 2 hours. Serve with custard or a good sweet sauce.

Bonita Pudding

2 eggs
2 lemons
¼ lb sugar
¼ oz gelatine

Dissolve gelatine in a teacup of water. Beat the yolk of eggs with the sugar. Add the lemon juice to the gelatine. When the mixture begins to set add the well beaten whites of eggs and put into a glass dish and decorate with cream.

Beeston Juice Pudding

¼ lb flour
2 oz suet
2 oz sugar
1 small teaspoon baking powder
1 egg well beaten
A little milk
Jam or stewed fruit

Put the fruit in a pie dish and pour mixture on the top and bake ½ hour.

Brandy Butter

¼ lb of butter
¼ lb of castor sugar and brandy to flavour.

Beat the butter to a cream. Gradually add the sugar and next the brandy drop by drop.

Bun Loaf

Mix ½ lb of butter with 2 lbs of flour
½ lb of sugar
½ lb of raisins

When stoned, some candied peel, ½ oz of soda. Mix the soda in a pint of milk. Beat all well together and put it in the oven immediately.

Castle Puddings

3 eggs, weight of eggs in flour, butter and sugar - the butter to be

melted. The yolks and whites of eggs to be beaten separately.

Butter small cups and half fill them. Bake in quick oven for 12 minutes.

Chartreuse of Bananas

About 6 bananas
A little clean jelly
6 leaves gelatine
A few pistachio nuts
¾ pint of good cream
1 oz castor sugar
½ teacup of cold water

Line a plain soufflé tin with clean jelly. Cut about 3 bananas into slices and entirely line the mould with them. Fill in any spaces there may be with blanched pistachio nuts. Set it all with a little jelly. Pass the 3 remaining bananas through a wire sieve. Dissolve the gelatine in the water, add the sugar to it and the juice of half a lemon. When the gelatine is cool, but not cold, add to it the cream. Whisk until stiff enough to stick to the whisk. Stir the gelatine in it, also banana. Turn into lined mould and when quite set, dip in warm water and turn out.

Chartreuse of Orange

6 oranges
¾ pint of cream
2 oz sugar
½ oz leaf gelatine
2 tablespoonfuls of water
¼ pint of orange jelly

Take 4 oranges, peel them, divide into slices, dip each slice in jelly leaf.

Charlotte Russe

¼ lb savoury biscuits
1 oz caster sugar
Sixpenny jar of cream
1 teaspoon vanilla or almond flavouring

Line the bottom of a plain mould with jelly and fit the biscuits all round the sides close together. Whisk the cream to a stiff froth. With the sugar and flavouring, add ¼ oz dissolved gelatine. Whisk and then pour into the mould.

Chocolate Cream

6 oz sugar
2 oz chocolate
12 drops vanilla
½ oz icing glass dissolved in a pint of milk
4 eggs well beaten

Whip a pint of essence firm and add the mixture to it - pour into a mould when nearly cold and stand till firm.

Chocolate Mould

1 pint of milk
3 oz of chocolate
3 oz of sugar
½ teaspoonful vanilla
2 eggs well beaten

Dissolve sugar and chocolate and icing glass in the milk and add the eggs when almost cold.

Choux Paste

1 oz butter
1 oz sugar
¼ pint water

2 ½ oz of sifted flour

Claret Jelly

½ pint water
½ pint claret
5 oz lump sugar
Rind and juice of 1 ½ lemons
1 oz gelatine
A little carmine
Whites of 2 eggs

Peel the lemon thinly and put the rind in a pan, with the water, gelatine and sugar. Stir until they are dissolved, then take off the fire and add the claret and lemon juice and the stiffly whisked whites of the eggs. Whisk well into the jelly, bring to a boil and keep boiling for 6 minutes. Pass through a jelly bag and when it has all run through, turn into a mould that has been rinsed well, in cold water.

Compote of Fruit

¼ pint of water
5 oz sugar boiled gently for 10 minutes

Then put in 1 lb of fruit and let it simmer until done, around quarter hour.

Crème de Banana

½ pint stiff orange jelly
4 bananas passed through a sieve
2 tablespoonfuls of apricot jam
A small glass of maraschino
A little carmine and sugar to taste

Rub bananas through wire sieve with a spoon, 1 pint of cream to decorate on. The top of jelly, when set in the dish, sprinkled with a few pistachio nuts. Add the banana pulp to the jelly before it sets, also the jam and maraschino, more sugar if needed, a little carmine to make a pretty red. When setting, pour in a glass or silver dish, allow it to set. When set pass the cream through a cake forcer on the top of it in heaps, piling high in the centre. Sprinkle over it the pistachio nuts.

Cumberland Pudding

2 oz flour
2 oz butter
2 oz sugar
2 eggs
2 rinds grated (of lemon)
1 pint milk

Melt the butter, add the flour and sugar, stir till smooth then add the boiling milk gradually and the grated lemon till a smooth sauce. Let it cool and add the yolk of egg and stir the whipped whites lightly in. Bake in a moderate oven ½ an hour.

Custard

1 pint of milk
1 pint of cream
A little sugar and lemon peel

Boil all together then pour gently the yolks of 8 eggs well beaten. Put it back in the pan, stir it over the fire, not to boil.

Custard II

½ pint of milk
Yolks of 3 eggs
3 oz castor sugar

De Grey Pudding

Take the weight of an egg in butter, fine sugar and flour. Beat the butter thoroughly to a cream. Add sugar, beat again, then the well beaten egg. Add a tiny bit of baking powder and a little chopped candied cherries and angelica. Steam sharply for 1 hour. Serve with custard sauce flavoured with sherry. Use one more egg, flour and sugar if a larger pudding is wanted. The above makes a nice pudding for 2 or more people.

Everton Toffee

1 lb sugar (½ loaf, ½ raw)
1 small teacupful of cold water
2 oz butter

Boil until hard and then add a few drops of essence of lemon. Pour into a well greased tin.

Free Kick Pudding

6 oz breadcrumbs
6 oz flour
6 oz of suet
6 oz raisins stoned
6 oz of currants
4 oz sugar
3 tablespoonfuls of treacle
Carbonate of soda

Steam 3 hours

French Pancakes

2 eggs
2 oz butter
2 oz sifted sugar
2 oz flour
½ pint of new milk

Beat the eggs thoroughly and put them into a basin with the butter, which should be beaten to a cream. Stir in the sugar and flour and when these ingredients are well mixed add the milk. Keep stirring and beating the mixture for a few minutes. Put it on buttered plates and bake in a quick oven for 20 minutes. Serve with a cut lemon.

French Pancakes II

2 oz butter
2 oz sugar
2 oz flour
2 eggs beaten up in ½ pint of milk

Work the butter to a cream, then add the castor sugar and stir for about 5 minutes, then add the flour. Mix all well together and stir in gradually the milk and eggs. bake in buttered sauces for 20 minutes. This quantity makes 5 pancakes.

Fritters

2 lb of flour
Rather more than a pint of new milk.
4 eggs well beaten, mixed with the milk
2 tablespoons of German yeast.
Currants and sugar to taste

It requires 1 ½ hours to rise, then fry in hot lard.

Fruit Loaf

2 lbs flour
½ lb butter
1 lb currants
1 lb raisins
2 oz peel
6 oz sugar
3 eggs and a little yeast

Rub the butter in the flour. Add the peel and cinnamon. Eggs and yeast dissolved in milk. Beat this to a light sponge and let it stand to size. When nicely risen add currants, raisins and sugar. Mix and bake from 2 to 3 hours.

Fruit Syrup

Dissolve 2 ½ oz of tartaric acid in one quart of water. Pour cold over 5 lbs fruit. Let it stand 24 hours. Strain through a sieve. Add 1 ½ lbs loaf sugar to 1 pint of juice. Let it stand 24 hours, stirring occasionally; then bottle, cork lightly; it will keep for years. This is made with any fruit or with oranges and lemons in slices. For jellies dissolve 1 oz gelatine in ½ pint of cold water. Then add half a pint of boiling water. When cooling stir in one pint of syrup.

Garnish for mould

Line a mould about ½ inch thick with lemon jelly, that has been coloured with carmine. Decorate according to taste.

Genoese Pastry

5 oz flour
5 oz sifted sugar
¼ lb butter
6 eggs
½ teaspoonful baking powder

Put the butter into a basin and beat it to a cream with a wooden spoon. Beat the eggs well and add them with the flour and sugar by degrees to the butter, beating well all the time. Now add the baking powder. Line the pastry tin with buttered paper; pour the mixture in and bake in a rather quick oven.

German Sweet

Fruit juice thickened with ground rice

About 1 large tablespoon of ground rice to a pint of juice

Mix the ground rice with a little water, then pour on the boiling juice. Return to the pan to thicken for a few minutes, sweeten to taste, serve in small glasses when cold. Very good made with raspberry or lemon juice.

Gingerbread Pudding

¼ lb bread crumbs
¼ lb suet
1 oz flour
6 oz treacle
1 teaspoonful ground ginger

Mix altogether and boil 2 hours.

Gingerbread Pudding II

¼ lb of suet
6 oz flour
2 oz of bread crumbs
1 teaspoon of baking powder
3 tablespoons of brown sugar
1 tablespoon of ground ginger
Pinch of salt
½ lb treacle
1 egg
A little milk

Mix the dry ingredients together, beat the egg. Add a little milk and mix the pudding with this and the treacle, working it well together with a wooden spoon. Well butter a mould. Put in the mixture and cover over with a greased paper and strain 2 ½ hours.

Gingerbread Sponge

1 lb flour

½ lb treacle or syrup
½ lb sugar granulated
3 oz margarine or lard
5 teaspoonfuls baking powder
1 teaspoon ground ginger
½ pint of milk

Put butter in and add the other ingredients. Mix quickly and bake in a shallow tin.

Half Pay Pudding

6 oz flour
6 oz bread crumbs
6 oz suet
6 oz currants
6 oz raisins
1 tablespoonful of treacle and a little milk

Boil 4 hours.

Hasty Pudding I

1 pint boiling milk
A little salt

Stir in gradually 2 oz flour and beat well. Add two eggs and put in the oven to brown on the top.

Hasty Pudding II

3 tablespoonfuls of flour
Salt
1 egg
1 pint milk

Make into a batter like Yorkshire pudding then boil the rest of the milk and pour over. Stir well and put back in the pan and boil for 5 minutes. Then put in the oven or under the gas grill to brown.

Honey Comb Mould

3 teacupfuls milk
1 small teacup loaf sugar
½ oz gelatine
3 eggs

Flavour with essence of almonds. Soak the gelatine in one cup of milk for an hour, then put the remainder of the milk with sugar and gelatine over the fire until discoloured. The yolks well beaten should then be added and kept well stirred over the fire until on the verge of boiling. Have the whites beaten to a stiff froth into which pour and stir quickly the milk and pour into well wetted mould and do not move until cold and set.

Jam Cockles

4 oz flour
4 oz cornflour
4 oz butter
4 oz castor sugar
1 egg
Grated rind of a lemon

Beat butter and sugar together. Add the other ingredients and drop on a greased baking sheet in teaspoonfuls. When baked a pale brown spread jam or jelly between and place one on top of the other. Bake in a moderate oven and the mixture must be largely stiff or it will run too much.

Jelson's Gelatine Jelly
(only one entry for "Jelson's gelatine" online)

Soak 1 oz gelatine in ½ pint of cold water for 2 or 3 hours then add ½ pint of boiling water. Mix until dissolved and add the juice and peel of 2 lemons, with wine and sugar sufficient to make the whole quantity 1 quart. Have ready the white and shell of an egg, well beaten together and mix these briskly into the jelly. Boil for 2 minutes without stirring it, remove from the fire. Allow it to stand 2 minutes and strain through a close flannel bag. Let it be nearly cold before pouring into the mould.

Junket

Take 1 ½ pints of milk and make ½ pint of it just blood warm. Put some brown sugar into a bowl and dissolve it with a wine glass of brandy. Then add the cold milk and eight drops of essence of almond, also some ratifias, if liked. Then add the warm milk and carry the bowl to a cool place, where it must remain untouched after the rennet is added. Add a tablespoonful of the prepared rennet and stir it well into the bowl, especially in the middle. Grate some nutmeg over the top. Cover it with a plate and leave it for an hour, when the curd will have formed.

Kissinger Pudding

2 oz whole rice
1 oz gelatine
1 pint of cream
1 pint custard
Sugar and vanilla

Cree (my 95-year-old grandmother confirmed for me that creed rice was pre-soaked rice) the rice in the pint of milk. Dissolve the gelatine in a little water. Beat the rice well, then add the custard and pint of whipped cream. Add the sugar and vanilla. Whisk all well together pouring in the gelatine. Pour into two moulds (pint size) ready garnished with crystallised cherries cut in two, or tinned apricots.

Lemon Cream

¾ pint of good cream
2 lemons

4 oz loaf sugar
6 leaves gelatine
½ teacup cold water

Rub the sugar on to the rind of the lemon and pound it, soak and dissolve gelatine in a pan with the water. Now add sugar and strained lemon juice. Allow the sugar to dissolve, whisk the cream until stiff. Now stir in the gelatine and lemon when cool, but not setting. When the cream shows signs of setting, turn into a mould rinsed in cold water and when set, dip in hot water and turn out.

N.B. The mould may be decorated if liked, with lemon jelly and crystallised fruits.

Lemon Curd

4 lemons
½ lb loaf sugar
½ lb butter
4 eggs

Put the butter and sugar into a double saucepan over boiling water and stir until the sugar has melted. Add rind and juice of lemons. Mix the yolk well with a fork and stir in. Cook, stirring, for about 20 minutes till the mixture thickens. It must not be allowed to boil. Pour into hot jars. Makes 2lb.

Lemon Mould

1 pint of water
2 lemons
2 eggs (yolks only)
6 oz loaf sugar
2 oz corn flour

Peel the lemons thinly and put the rind into a saucepan with most of the water and the sugar and let it slowly come to a boil. Mix the corn flour smoothly with the rest of the water. Squeeze the juice of the lemons into the pan as long as it has boiled a moment and strain all over the corn flour. Add the yolks of the eggs and mix, turning all back into the pan. Stir until it boils 2 or 3 minutes, stirring all the time. Then pour into a wetted mould, and dish out when perfectly cold.

Lemon Sponge

4 lemons
1 oz gelatine
1 lb caster sugar
4 eggs (whites only)

Squeeze the lemons into a bowl. Add the whites of the eggs and the caster sugar. Dissolve the gelatine in breakfast cups of cold water. When a pure liquid add to the zest, and whisk all for 20 minutes. Put into a mould in a cool place. Add one more egg to the yolks for custard.

Meringues

Take a baking tin, warm it and grease with white wax. Whisk 4 whites of eggs very stiff, now quickly and lightly whisk in ½ oz of very fine castor sugar. Place with desert spoon on the tin in pieces the size of an egg. Dust well over with icing sugar. Bake in a very slow oven until the top is set. Loosen from the tin, and holding each meringue in your hand press the bottom of it with a small egg. Now return to the oven to make crisp and when cold fill with whipped cream.

Meringues a la Francaise

The whites of 3 fresh eggs
6 oz best castor sugar

Whisk the eggs to a very stiff froth, then stir into them very quickly and lightly the sugar. Warm a tin and rub it all over with white wax. Put the mixture into a bag with a plain pipe and pass it out on to the waxed tin, in the shape of small round baskets. Dredge them well with icing and sugar and put them into a cool place and let them remain till they are quite dry and set. Great care must be taken that they do not get coloured. When they are wanted for use, decorate them, by filling them with whipped cream and put on the top, little pieces of glace cherries and angelica. Cut a very thin strip of angelica to form a handle on each meringue.

Mince Meat

2 ½ lb currants
2 lb sultanas & raisins
2 lb brown sugar
¼ lb mixed peel
½ lb cooking almonds
2 oz bitter almonds
12 large apples finely chopped
3 large lemons (rind and juice)

Mince Meat II

2 lb suet
2 lb Valencia raisins chopped
2 lb apples
2 lb currants
6 tablespoonfuls marmalade
2 lb brown sugar
¾ lb chopped almonds
4 lemons (rind and juice)
A little candied peel
Brandy

Mousseline Pudding

2 oz butter
2 ½ oz castor sugar
The rind of 2 lemons, grated
The juice of one lemon and the yolks of 5 eggs

Stir over the fire until thick, but it must not boil. Whisk the whites of the eggs to a stiff froth and stir lightly into the mixture, pour into a plain charlotte mould that has been buttered and dusted over with fine sugar and flour mixed and steam for 40 minutes. Let it stand for about 3 minutes before turning out.

 Sauce for above:

2 ½ yolks of eggs
1 wineglass maraschino or sherry
The whites of 2 eggs
1 ½ oz castor sugar

Stand the pan in another pan with boiling water and stir with a whisk till the contents are stiff like a soufflé.

Orange Chartreuse

½ pint of clear jelly
6 sweet oranges
¾ pint of cream
6 leaves of gelatine
½ teacup of water
3 oz of sugar
1 oz pistachio nuts

Line a tin mould with the jelly, put two oranges on one side to use for the cream. Take the peel and white pith from the rest of the oranges and cut into very small quarters. Line the mould with them, fill in the spaces with the chopped nuts set with jelly. Rub the sugar on to the rind of one of the oranges. Pound and dissolve in the juice of the two. Melt the gelatine in the water. Whisk the cream until stiff. Now add first the gelatine, then the syrup and when beginning to set, then turn into lined mould until quite set.

Orange Jelly

1 oz gelatine
6 oranges

½ lb loaf sugar
1 pint cold water
2 lemons

Rub sugar on to rind of two oranges and 1 lemon. Soak gelatine in water till dissolved. Put gelatine, water and sugar in a pan and stir. Until sugar is dissolved, add juice from oranges and lemons. Just bring to a boil and then pour gently through a piece of muslin and when getting cool, put into mould which has been rinsed in cold water.

Pancake Scones

2 teacups of flour
½ teaspoonful carbonate of soda
1 teaspoonful cream of tartar
½ teaspoonful salt
1 teaspoonful of syrup
1 teaspoonful of butter (melted)
½ teacupful of sugar (small)
1 egg (well beaten)

Mix carefully to a smooth thin batter with milk (thick as cream) so that it will run. Grease the griddle and make it hot, then pour mixture in tablespoonfuls on griddle and turn once.

Patriotic Pudding

2 oz margarine
4 oz flour
¼ pint milk
Salt
2 oz sugar
1 egg
1 teaspoonful baking powder
3 tablespoonful syrup

Line a basin with the syrup. Mix all the ingredients well together. Pour into the basin, steam 2 hours.

Plum Pudding

1 ½ lb bread crumbs
1 lb currants
½ lb raisins (stoned)
2 oz mixed peel
2 grated carrots
½ lb raw sugar
4 eggs
¼ lb suet and a little milk

Steam two hours. Will make two small puddings.

Potato Pudding

6 medium potatoes, steamed and mashed with a teaspoonful of flour. 1 gill of milk or cream, sugar to taste. A little grated lemon rind or a spoonful of marmalade. 2 eggs well beaten. Bake in a moderate oven.

Puffed Paste

(for 12 patties)
½ lb butter
½ lb flour
2 teaspoonfuls lemon juice
¼ pint cold water

Press the butter lightly in the corner of a floured cloth. Then rub 2 oz of it into the flour. Add the lemon juice and cold water to this to mix into a stiff paste. Roll it out into a thick piece and put the lump of butter in the centre and fold the paste well over and roll out into a long piece. Then flour, fold in three and roll out again. Do this once more and put it away for 2 hours. Then roll out twice more and let it stand ½ an hour longer, then roll out twice more and it is ready to bake. The patty cases should be ¼ of an inch thick. Cut the cases out with a round cutter and take a much smaller cutter and just mark the centre. Bake them in a quick oven - and take out the small rim of paste and scoop out the centre and fill with the mixture and replace with a lid. The paste should be rolled 7 times in all.

Raspberry Pudding

2 eggs
The weight of 2 eggs in butter
Caster sugar and flour
2 small tablespoons raspberry jam
½ small teaspoon carbonate soda
2 teaspoon milk

Beat the butter to a cream, add sugar and beat together. Beat eggs and mix in with flour. Then add jam and lastly soda dissolved in milk. Turn into greased mould or cups and steam 1 ½ hours. Use custard sauce.

Raspberry Sandwich

¼ lb butter (cream it)
¼ lb caster sugar
¼ lb flour
2 eggs
1 teaspoonful baking powder

Bake in a quick oven.

Raspberry Sandwich II

2 oz butter
2 oz sugar
3 oz flour
1 teaspoonful baking powder
2 eggs
Grated rind of a lemon

Bake quickly in a buttered tin lined with paper.

Rhubarb Cream

1 ½ lbs rhubarb
½ pint cold water
½ lb loaf sugar
½ pint cream
1 good teaspoonful of sugar
¾ oz gelatine
A little cochineal
½ teacup of cold water in addition to half a pint

Wipe and cut up the rhubarb. Put in a pan with half pint of water, bring to a boil and simmer until tender. Now strain it, add the sugar, bring to a boil and skim. Let it boil till clear, now allow to get quite cold. Dissolve the gelatine in the half cup of water. Whisk up the cream until stiff, add the sugar before whisking. Stir in about ½ pint of the syrup and the gelatine mixture, which should be cool. Stir until just beginning to set. Now turn into a mould rinsed out with cold water. When set a little of the syrup, if liked, may be poured round the mould may be lined first with jelly (red).

Rhubarb Mould

Take 1 quart of rhubarb, cut it into short lengths and stew it till quite a pulp. Dissolve ½ an ounce of gelatine and put with it ¾ lb of sugar. Put these to the rhubarb and boil for a quarter of an hour. Pour into a mould and serve with custard poured round.

Rice Cheesecakes

¼ lb butter
¼ lb sugar
¼ lb ground rice
Yolks of 2 eggs and white of one. A few drops of essence of almonds.

Rice Cream

1 ½ oz ground rice swelled in 1 pint new milk over the fire until thick like cream; then sent to cool. Dissolve ½ oz icing glass or gelatine in a very little more milk. Whip up very stiff ½ pint of good cream; add 4 oz sifted sugar, then mix in the rice a spoonful at a time and lastly add the icing glass - mix well and mould directly. Serve with raspberry syrup.

Royal Cream

1 pint milk
2 eggs
1 large tablespoonful fine sugar
7 sheets gelatine (whole sheets)
2 tablespoonfuls sherry

Soak the gelatine in milk ½ hour. Beat the yolks and sugar 10 minutes. Put all in a double saucepan till nearly boiling, stirring well. Cool and add stiffly whipped whites of egg and put in a 3 gill mould.

Russian Cream

Mix a large tablespoonful cornflour
The yolks of 2 eggs
A little grated lemon
2 oz butter with a little cold milk

Then pour 1 pint of boiling milk on it, return to the pan and boil for 2 minutes. Pour into a soufflé dish or small cases. When cold put a thick layer of brown sugar and brown with a salamander and serve cold.

Scones

6 oz flour
2 oz shortening

Pinch of salt
Dessert spoon baking powder
2 oz sultanas and currants mixed
1 oz candied peel
1 teaspoonful of sugar

Scotch Girdle Scones

1 oz of flour
1 dessertspoonful of butter
½ teaspoonful cream of tartar
½ teaspoonful carbonate of soda drenched in milk
A pinch of salt and sugar

Mix with warm milk into a stiff paste. Bake on a hot floured griddle and turn scones once only.

Short Pastry Mushrooms
(by "mushrooms" I believe they mean tarts)

¼ lb of flour
2 oz butter
½ teaspoonful of castor sugar
If liked richer, you may add the yolk of an egg

Rub the butter lightly into the flour, add sugar, egg and cold water, to mix quite stiff. Roll out about twice or until it is quite smooth. Line some patty tins with some of the paste. Put a piece of bread in each or a buttered paper with raw rice. Prick the bottom of tartlets, roll out the trimming rather thin. Cut into strips and roll them up to make little stacks for the mushrooms. Bake in a quick oven for 15 minutes. Have ready some whipped cream and when the pastry is cold, fill the patty tins with whipped cream. Dust them over with grated chocolate or cocoa, stick the stacks in and they are ready. A little apricot jam might be put at the bottom of the tartlets, then cream.

Small Cold Chocolate Soufflé

½ pint of milk
1 oz sugar
4 leaves of gelatine
2 eggs
1 ½ oz chocolate
Essence of vanilla

Make the milk hot, melt the gelatine in it, pour over the yolks of eggs. While in the pan to thicken, when just beginning to set add ½ a pint of whipped cream, (or if not required so thick ¼ pint) then the stiffly beaten whites of eggs. Pour quickly into soufflé cases, which have a round of paper round them to come ½ an inch higher than the case. When set decorate with biscuit crumbs or whipped cream, pistachio chopped fine etc.

Small Cold Raspberry Soufflé

Raspberry made the same way (refers to chocolate soufflé). Raspberries pulped through a sieve. To make one teacupful you want only ½ the quantity of milk or custard. The raspberry pulp must not be added until cold. Apples or gooseberries soufflé made the same way.

Soda Pudding

6 oz flour
3 oz chopped suet grated
3 oz sugar
3 oz currants
3 oz raisins
1 oz candied peel
A little salt
½ a teacup of milk
1 tablespoonful of treacle
¼ of a teaspoonful baking powder
1 egg
½ a teaspoon carbonate soda

Carbonate of soda, treacle and baking powder to be mixed with the milk. When made put into a well wetted mould and steam or boil 3 hours.

Spanish Puffs

Boil ¾ pint of milk with 2 oz butter. 6 oz flour stirred into the boiling milk. Flavour with vanilla. Drop about the size of a walnut and bake lightly. When done, open gently at the side and fill with jam.

Sponge Custard Mould

1 pint of milk
1 large or 2 small eggs
½ oz gelatine
2 tablespoonfuls caster sugar
Flavour to taste with vanilla

Method: Heat the milk and stir into it well beaten yolks and sugar. Return to the pan till it thickens. Melt the soaked gelatine by adding a tablespoonful of boiling water and standing in a pan of hot water. When melted add it to the thickened milk, mix, flavour and let to cool. When it begins to congeal, whisk it thoroughly with an egg beater, adding to it gradually the white of an egg beaten stiff. Beat rapidly till quite spongy. Fill a quart mould with it, a little sherry to flavour, or brandy.

Sponge Pudding

3 eggs, their weight in flour, sugar, and butter.

Beat the butter to a cream, heat the eggs and mix all well together, a little grated lemon rind. Butter a mould and sift with sugar. Steam 1 hour.

Sponge Sandwich

3 oz self raising flour
1 oz cornflour
4 oz margarine
4 oz granulated sugar
2 eggs
Jam
Bake for about 35 minutes

Sultana Pudding

Take 2 eggs and their weight in castor sugar, butter and flour
3 oz sultanas
1 small teaspoonful baking powder

Beat the butter to a cream. Add the sugar, the beaten eggs and lastly the raisins picked, the flour and baking powder. Turn into a greased mould, cover with greased paper and steam for an hour and a half.
You can turn this into a raspberry pudding by putting 2 tablespoonfuls of jam instead of the raisins. Sultana in tin mould. Raspberry in pot mould. Serve with arrowroot sauce.

Supreme De Crème

Put a little lemon jelly or any other, at the bottom of mould to decorate and a few glazed cherries as well
½ oz leaf gelatine (Mrs Marshall's)
½ a teacup of cold water.

Dissolve the gelatine in the water, add to that the wine brandy and lemon juice. 4 oz glazed cherries or mixed fruits, chopped a little, 3 oz loaf sugar, 1 lemon, 3 tablespoonfuls of sherry, 1 tablespoonfuls of brandy. Whisk the cream until rather stiff and now add the gelatine rather hot. Carefully the rind of the lemon must be rubbed on the sugar. Stir in the chopped fruit into the cream when it is getting stiff and when it will bear the fruit it is ready to mould. ¾ pint of cream.

Supreme et Crème

¾ pint cream
3 oz lump sugar
3 oz glace fruits
1 small lemon
3 tablespoons sherry
1 ½ tablespoons of brandy
6 leaves of gelatine
½ teacup cold water

The sugar must be rubbed on to the rind of the lemon and then pounded. Dissolve the gelatine in the water, then add the sugar, brandy and sherry and the lemon juice. Whip the cream till stiff, then add the liquid ingredients and lastly the cut up fruits. When the cream shows signs of setting, turn into the garnished mould.

Swiss Roll Pudding

2 eggs
½ breakfast cup castor sugar (food measure)
½ breakfast cup flour
A little baking powder.

Beat the eggs well, then add sugar and mix well then flour and lastly a very little baking powder. Turn into a well greased tin lined with paper, and bake in a fairly, but not too hot, oven. When done trim the edges neatly off. Spread with raspberry jam, and roll up at once and sift sugar over and serve.

Swiss Roll

2 eggs
2 ½ oz castor sugar
2 oz self raising flour
1 desertspoonful warm water

Swiss Roll II

2 eggs
3 oz castor sugar
2 oz flour
1 tablespoonful milk
½ teaspoonful baking powder

Beat the eggs with the sugar
Add the flour

Dissolve baking powder in the milk and add the other ingredients. Butter a small baking tin, and pour in the mixture. Bake in a quick oven 10 minutes. Turn out in a paper dredged with castor sugar, and spread with jam and roll.

Swiss Roll III

1 teacup flour
1 oz sugar
1 oz butter
1 egg
1 teaspoon baking powder
Jam

Warm the jam. Melt sugar and butter, add warm flour.

Tea Raspberries

To 1 lb of raspberries put 18 oz sugar

Let the sugar remain on the fruit over night. Then squeeze with the hand till no lumps remain. Put in the pan till it comes to the boil. Take up and lie while hot. Squeeze a little before putting in the sugar.

Velvet Creams

Soak ½ oz gelatine in a quarter of pint of water for half an hour.

Pour upon it ¼ pint cherry or raisin wine and return it over the fire till dissolved. Add 4 oz of loaf sugar which have been rubbed upon the rind of 2 fresh lemons together with a tablespoonful of lemon juice. Return the mixture over the fire till the sugar is dissolved. Pour the liquor into a bowl. When it is cool mix with it gradually but thoroughly a pint of thick cream. Pour into a mould, which has been raised out with cold water.

Vermoise Pudding

1 ½ pints of milk
1 ½ oz arrowroot
¼ oz gelatine
2 eggs
Sugar and flavouring to taste
3 or 4 sponge cakes

Line a quart mould with sponge cakes. Soak with raisin wine. Take 1 pint of the milk and out of it take a little to mix the arrowroot to a thick cream. Let the remainder of the pint come nearly to a boil for about 2 minutes. Take off the fire and stir in the whites of eggs stiffly beaten. Pour into mould with the sponge cakes in. Serve cold with custard poured over (with the ½ pint of milk and 2 yolks make some custard).

Vermoise Pudding II

5 oz bread cut in small squares
3 oz caster sugar
1 oz loaf sugar
1 lemon
¾ pint of milk
3 oz sultana raisins
1 oz mixed nuts and dried fruits
A few pistachios
Yolks of 4 eggs

Cut the bread without crust in small squares, grate the lemon rind. Put all the dry ingredients together. Put the loaf sugar "broken" into a brass pan. Let it get quite brown, then pour the milk on to it. Stir well. Beat yolks of eggs, put all ingredients into a basin. Butter and decorate a mould and pour all in. Steam 2 hours. Better cold than hot.

Wheatmeal Pudding

6 oz wheatmeal
3 oz treacle
3 oz sugar
2 oz butter, margarine or dripping
1 teaspoon baking powder
Salt
Rind of lemon
1 egg or milk

Milk to mix to a batter, put into greased basin, steam 2 hours.

Whipped Cream

½ pint of cream
1 oz caster sugar
A little vanilla

Add the sugar to the cream and whip until stiff.

Whipped Cream II

¼ pint good cream
½ oz castor sugar
A few drops essence of vanilla

**Recipes mentioned by title but without ingredients or cooking instructions were:

Puddings Hot:

Viennese Pudding, Cabinet Pudding, Chocolate Pudding, Coconut Pudding, Vanilla Soufflé, Chocolate Soufflé, Apple Soufflé, Little Marie Pudding

Cold Pudding:

Bakewell Pudding, Caramel Pudding, Diplomatic Pudding, Mocha Pudding, Gateau d' Ananas.

Jellies:

Lemon Jelly, Orange Jelly, Wine Jelly, Coffee Jelly, Apricot Jelly, Jelle a la Belfranc, Claret Jelly, Jelie Dantifie, Marischino Jelly

Cakes and Biscuits

Alexandra Cake

3 oz flour
2 oz butter
3 oz sugar
½ teaspoonful baking powder
2 eggs

Cream the butter, add sugar, then eggs. Colour half with cochineal. Turn into a flat tin, lined with buttered paper and bake in a moderate oven until quite set. When cool, remove paper and lay quite flat on a cake rest. When quite cold, spread one with a layer of almond icing and put the other colour on top and cover with white icing. Cut in fancy shapes.

Almond Cakes

Rub 2 oz of butter into 5 oz flour.
5 oz caster sugar

Beat an egg with half the sugar then put it to the other.
1 oz ground almonds and a little essence of almonds.

Roll in your hands the size of a nutmeg and sprinkle with sugar and bake lightly.

Almond Cheesecakes

2 tablespoonfuls almond ground
2 tablespoonfuls of sugar
1 gill milk

Almond Fingers

Make Shortbread:

6 oz flour
2 oz sugar
2 oz rice flour
4 oz butter

Press this shortbread into a shallow oblong tin (like welsh cake tin).
Spread a thin layer of jam over and put on the following mixture:

2 tablespoons ground almonds
3 tablespoons castor sugar
1 tablespoon ground rice
1 egg
Chopped almonds on top and bake in a slow oven

Almond Icing

Mix 1lb of almond meal with 1lb caster sugar. The stiffly beaten
whites (and yolks) of 2 eggs. A little almond flavouring. Knead well
with the hand.

Baba rum

2 eggs
2 oz castor sugar
2 oz melted butter
2 oz flour
1 teaspoonful baking powder

Beat together 2 eggs and sugar. Add melted butter, flour and baking
powder. Bake half an hour. Put into saucepan and bring to boil two
tablespoonfuls of water and two of rum and 12 lumps of loaf sugar
and pour over pudding. Bake in casserole mould with hole in centre,
which when serving fill with fruit or whipped cream.

Biscuits

½ lb of flour

¼ lb of butter
½ lb of sugar
1 egg and a little almond flavouring

Black Biscuits

1 lb flour
½ lb caster sugar
½ lb butter
2 eggs and a few currants

Beat the butter by itself, beat the eggs and mix them with butter and sugar, add flour and currants and take out with a fork and drop mixture onto baking tray, about the size of walnuts.

Bourneville Cake

2 eggs
2 oz castor sugar
2 oz fine flour
½ teaspoonful of baking powder
Vanilla

Stir the yolks of eggs with sugar, for five minutes, then add the whites, beaten to a stiff froth, flour, baking powder and vanilla. When nicely mixed pour into a tin lined with buttered paper and bake 20 minutes. When cold cut in two and lay a layer of icing between the two pieces. Cover the cake all over with icing and make it smooth with knife dipped in hot water.

Brown Plum Cake

1 ¼ lb flour
½ lb chopped peel
2 lb currants
1 lb castor sugar
2 grated nutmegs
12 eggs

2 lbs stoned raisins
1 lb butter
1 oz cinnamon
2 teaspoonfuls baking powder
1 ½ wine glass brandy

Beat butter and sugar to a cream. Add eggs and flour alternately. Having already prepared fruit, add it to mixture, add brandy last of all and give it a good beat up. Bake in moderate oven till firm in centre about 3 hours. Ice on top the usual way. 3 eggs to 1 lb of almonds ground.

Buols French Cakes

½ lb flour
½ lb sugar
½ lb butter
½ lb ground almonds

Work butter and sugar well together. Mix almonds and flour steadily with it.

Cake

½ lb butter
½ lb sugar
5 eggs
½ lb currants
¼ lb candied peel
A little baking powder

Beat the butter to a cream. Add the sugar, then add the eggs one by one, then the currants, candied peel and 12 oz flour. Bake for an hour and a half in a moderate oven.

Cake II

½ lb apricot jam

¼ pint of water
1 tablespoonful of brown sugar
½ quantity makes a nice sized cake.

Cheesecakes

½ lb curd
3 eggs
2 oz sugar
2 oz currants
A little candied peel
A little brandy

Line mould tins with pastry and put the mixture in and bake till set.

Children's Cakes

1 breakfast cup flour
½ breakfast cup sugar

Butter the size of a walnut rubbed in:
1 teaspoonful baking powder
2 tablespoonfuls of milk

Chocolate Buns

3 oz flour, sugar and butter.
2 oz grated chocolate and mixed with the yolks of 2 eggs with which a teaspoonful of vanilla essence has been beaten. Put on a baking sheet about the size of a walnut and bake 10 minutes.

Chocolate Cake

¼ lb butter
2 oz caster sugar
2 oz grated chocolate
3 oz flour

2 eggs
½ teaspoonful baking powder

Beat the butter to a cream. Add the chocolate, beat well together (with wooden spoon). Now put in the sugar, then eggs and flour. Mix all together and bake in a moderate oven 20 minutes. Line the tin with buttered paper. When cold ice it over.

Icing

¼ lb icing sugar to 1 oz of chocolate.

Chocolate Éclairs

2 oz butter
2 oz sugar
¼ pint of water
1 large or 2 small eggs
2 ½ oz flour

Place the butter and water in a saucepan until the butter is melted. When they boil, add the flour, and stir well in until quite smooth and cook for 1 or 2 minutes. Turn into a basin to get a little cool then add the well beaten eggs. Beat all well together. Place this into a forcing bag with a plain tube to force into finger lengths on a baking sheet and bake in a slow oven until nicely brown and cooked through. Then open the éclairs at one side, and fill with whipped cream, jam or thick custard and dip in chocolate icing.

Chocolate Icing

4 oz icing sugar (put through a fine sieve)
2 oz grated chocolate
A little water, about 2 tablespoonfuls.
Stir the icing over the fire for a minute or two and then dip in the éclairs.

Chocolate Icing II

½ lb icing sugar
2 oz chocolate
2 tablespoons boiling water

Mix together in a pan or basin, until it turns easily from the spoon and pour over the cake quickly.

Chocolate Icing III

4 oz icing sugar
2 oz fresh butter
A little essence of vanilla
½ oz Cadburys cocoa essence

Stir butter, sugar and vanilla to a cream. Add cocoa by degrees, sufficient to flavour and colour nicely.

Citron Cake

½ lb butter
½ lb eggs
½ lb sugar
½ lb flour
½ lb ground rice
1 oz Jordan almonds (also known as sugared almonds)

Citron on top of cake. Seed cake the same. 1 oz seeds rather than almonds.

Coconut Biscuits

1 teacupful of flour
1 teacupful sugar
2 teacupfuls desiccated coconut
As much white of egg as will mix it.

Drop on a well buttered tin small pieces.

Coconut or Almond Biscuits

4 oz desiccated coconut or 4 oz ground almonds
1 ½ oz fine sugar
The white of an egg.

Bake in a very slow oven.

Coffee Icing

½ oz icing sugar passed through a hair sieve
2 tablespoons very strong coffee
Mix with sugar made first warm over the fire and use at once.

Currant Yeast Cake

1 lb flour
1 lb sugar
1 lb currants
½ lb butter or margarine
1 tablespoonful baking powder
¼ lb candied peel
¾ oz yeast
1 gill warm milk
2 eggs
1 grated lemon

Rub the butter into the flour. Crumble the yeast in then mix altogether and put it into the tins and set to rise ½ hour by the fire before baking. Will make 3 small cakes.

Domino Cake

½ lb butter
½ lb sugar
½ lb flour
4 eggs

Icing
2 oz caster sugar
1 egg yolk
¼ lb powdered almonds

Make as Genoise pastry, divide the mixture into two, pick one half and bake in a small fat dripping tin lined with buttered paper, then when cold cut into strips ½ an inch thick, 4 of pink and 5 of plain cake. Place then the first 3 of the pink in the middle, second 3 the white strips in the middle, 3rd row the pink in the middle, stick them together with apricot jam, when the cake is formed spread the jam all over the cake and wrap up in almond icing as follows: Mix the almonds, sugar and the yolk of egg to a stiff paste, roll out and fold the cake in it.

Eccles Cakes

4 oz currants
 2 oz sugar
1 ½ oz butter
1 oz candied peel

Clean the currants. Melt butter in a pan, add sugar and currants and cook over the fire until hot and sugar allowed to partly melt. Roll out flaky pastry into small rounds. Put some of the mixture in each and fold over and press down with rolling pin. Brush with egg, sugar and prick with fork. Put on sheet and bake in fairly quick oven.

Eccles Cakes II

1 ½ oz butter
¼ oz finely chopped peel
2 oz sugar
4 oz currants

Melt butter and sugar in a saucepan, add peel, currants, until just hot and butter melted. Allow to cool on a plate.

Éclairs

1 ½ gill water
½ pint cream
2 ½ oz butter
1 tsp vanilla essence
2 eggs
3 oz caster sugar
3 ½ oz of flour
Chocolate Icing

Lightly grease a baking sheet. Put the butter in pan and bring to boil then add the flour all at once, cook till it leaves the pan clear. Let it cool then put in the beaten egg…(recipe incomplete in book)

Ginger Biscuits

1 lb flour
1 lb caster sugar
½ lb butter beaten to a cream
½ oz ginger
2 oz candied lemon
2 eggs and a tablespoon of cream

Ginger Cake

(½ quantity makes a nice layered cake)

10 oz flour
6 oz butter
4 oz brown sugar
2 oz candied peel
2 teaspoonfuls of ginger
½ oz baking powder
2 eggs
6 oz of golden syrup

Rub the butter into the flour. Add dry ingredients, mix well together, beat the eggs, add to the cake and lastly the syrup and 2 tablespoonfuls of milk. Bake in a moderate oven.

Ginger Cake II

3 small eggs
6 oz brown sugar
6 oz flour
3 oz butter melted
2 tablespoonful syrup
2 oz lemon peel cut fine
3 tablespoonfuls sultanas
½ oz ground ginger
Pinch of salt

Mix the dry ingredients together. Then add eggs, well whisked butter and syrup, beat well. Add ½ teaspoonful baking powder. Bake 1 hour in a moderate oven. This mixture will make small cakes.

Ginger Cake III

1 lb sugar
1 lb flour
½ lb butter
6 eggs
1 teacupful milk
2 teaspoons baking powder
1 or 2 tablespoons ginger syrup
Preserved ginger cut up in pieces

Beat butter and sugar together. Add yolks of eggs, one at a time, beating well. Then add the whites beaten to a stiff froth. Beat well together, add rest of ingredients without much further beating. Ice when cold and decorate with crystallised ginger.

Ginger Nuts

5 oz flour

2 oz butter
2 oz castor sugar
Teaspoonful ground ginger
¼ teaspoonful carbonate soda
1 ½ tablespoonfuls of treacle
A very little water

Beat butter to a cream. With the sugar add treacle, flour and ginger.
Mix the soda in a little water and add to the other ingredients. Make
into a stiff paste and form into small pieces the size of a large nut.
Bake in a moderate oven a nice brown.

Gingerbread

10 oz self raising flour
4 oz butter
4 oz Demerara sugar
2 eggs
½ gill of milk
2 tablespoons dark treacle
1 tablespoon golden syrup
1 tablespoon marmalade
1 teaspoon ground ginger
½ teaspoon ground rice

Bake 40 or 50 minutes in a moderate oven.

Gingerbread Parkin

12 oz flour
6 oz sugar
3 oz butter
½ lb treacle
2 teaspoonfuls baking powder
2 tablespoonfuls ground ginger
½ pint milk
2 eggs

Bake in small tins in a bread oven.

Girdle cakes

1 lb flour
¼ lb butter
1 teaspoonful baking powder
Enough thick cream or milk to make into a stiff paste

Rub butter well into flour. Add a pinch of salt and baking powder then mix and just roll out smooth and cut with a cutter into little cakes. Bake on the girdle turning occasionally to prevent burning. Half this quantity will make a good many cakes.

Honeycomb Gingerbread

¼ lb butter
¼ lb castor sugar
¼ lb best golden syrup
¼ lb flour
½ teaspoonful ground ginger

Put the butter, sugar and treacle into a pan on the fire and when the butter is melted and the sugar quite dissolved, let it boil for about a minute. Have the flour and ginger well mixed together in a basin. Then add the hot mixture and stir all together. Drop in small quantities on to a greased tin and bake in a moderate oven, till a pale golden colour. Take it out and let it remain till it is just beginning to set. Then toast each one round the handle of a wooden spoon or a stick for the purpose. It can also be poured on the greased tin and cut out with a round cutter.

Icing

The whites of 2 eggs and ½ lb sugar.

Jordan Cakes

1 ½ teacups flour
1 teacup caster sugar
Butter
The yoke of an egg
2 eggs
1 teaspoon cream of tartar
1 carbonate soda
2 tablespoons of milk

Mix well together and put a little into tins and bake in a moderate oven. Rub in the butter. When cold split and spread with raspberry juice.

Layer Cake

½ lb butter
½ lb caster sugar
½ lb flour
4 eggs

Beat butter to a cream. Add other ingredients in ordinary way. Bake in thin round layers in quick oven. When cold spread each layer with different kind of jam and place them one on the top of the other. Ice the whole cake with icing and decorate the top.

Layer Cake II

½ lb butter
½ lb sugar
6 oz flour
2 oz cornflour
5 eggs
1 teaspoons baking powder
Sherry or almond flavouring

Beat butter and sugar well, add 1 yolk at a time with the flour and cornflour. Whisk whites stiff and add with the flavouring. Bake in 4 tins (sandwich) and cut in layers. Spread with jam or icing. Half the quantity makes a nice cake.

Lemon for Cheesecakes

4 oz butter
1 oz caster sugar
6 eggs, leaving out 2 whites
2 lemon rinds grated and the juice

Put into a jar and boil in a pan of water until it is like cream.

Madeira Cake

½ lb flour
Sugar
Butter and eggs
Cream

Mix sugar, eggs and flour. Add 1 teaspoonful baking powder. Beat well and bake about ¾ of an hour. Will make 2 small cakes.

Madeira or Cherry Cake

6 oz butter
6 oz castor sugar
10 oz flour
4 eggs
A small teaspoonful baking powder

Beat the butter to a cream. Add the sugar, then the beaten eggs. Lastly flour and baking powder. Turn into a tin lined with buttered paper and bake in a moderate oven for an hour and a quarter. It will do without baking powder. Quarter the cherries and allow 4 oz for every ½ oz flour used in the cake. Also can be added a little cherry essence or 1 oz chopped almonds. Ice and decorate with cherries and angelica.

Marbled Cake

2 teacupfuls moist sugar
3 teacupfuls flour
1 teacupful full milk
3 eggs
6 oz butter
3 oz chocolate
1 teaspoonful baking powder
1 teaspoonful essence vanilla
1 teaspoonful cochineal

Cream the butter and sugar. Mix in the yolks of eggs, then flour, baking powder and milk and well heat. Add next: the whites of eggs, beaten to a stiff froth and lastly vanilla. Divide the mixture into 3 parts: to one add chocolate, to the second, cochineal, and leave the third plain. Line a cake tin with buttered paper and drop the mixture in by Spoonfuls. Bake in a slow oven about 1 ½ hours.

Neapolitan Biscuit Cake

½ lb flour
6 oz sugar
1 egg
4 oz butter
2 oz ground almond
1 tablespoon cream

Mix and roll out very thin. Add to one of the pieces 1 oz chocolate powder, a little vanilla essence. Make into pieces of paste. Roll out about 6 pieces, cut with a large cutter. Bake in a moderate oven. When cold they look like large biscuits. Put a little apricot jam or glaze between each and put the colours alternately. Cut out small rings of glaze and glace cherries to decorate the top which can have a hole in the centre if liked, for whipped cream. Half the quantity makes a nice layered cake.

Glaze:
½ lb apricot jam
¼ pint water
1 tablespoonful of brown sugar

Neapolitan Cake

Make a sponge cake with:
The weight of 2 eggs in butter, sugar and flour
2 eggs

Bake ¾ of an hour or rather more. When cold stamp out the inside then soak in a little rum. Cover with apricot-jam. Decorate with pieces, cut from inside of cake, cut into strips, with a crystallised cherry in each and grated pistachio, nuts and angelica and fill up the centre of cake with whipped cream.

Orange Cake

4 oz flour
½ teaspoonful of baking powder
Grated rind of 1 orange
Juice of 1 ½ oranges
6 oz of sifted sugar
3 or 4 oz butter
3 eggs

Cream the sugar and eggs together with a wooden spoon, adding the butter slightly melted. When thick and smooth add the rind and juice of oranges. Beat lightly then put in the flour and baking powder (well mixed). Lastly the well beaten whites of the eggs. This will make 2 nice small cakes. Line the tins with paper and bake 20 to 30 minutes. Cover when cold and set with soft icing, mixed with the juice of an orange. Glace apricot cut in small pieces and pistachio nuts in very small bits look pretty.

Parkin

4 oz coarse oatmeal
4 oz fine oatmeal
2 oz butter
½ pound treacle
½ teaspoonful of ground ginger

¼ teaspoonful of baking powder

Beat the butter to a cream, and then add the treacle and the oatmeal mixed, and a ¼ teaspoonful of baking powder the last thing. Then bake for a ¼ of an hour.

Plum Cake

1 lb flour
1 lb butter
1 lb sugar
1 ½ lb currants
½ lb sultanas
½ lb almonds
½ lb minced peel
8 eggs

A very little cinnamon, about as much as would lay on a sixpence. Grated lemon. Bake 5 hours carefully in a moderate oven.

Plum Cake for France

1 oz butter or margarine
1 oz sugar
1 ½ oz flour
6 oz peel
1 ½ oz currants
5 eggs
1 teaspoonful baking powder
A little pinch of salt

Cream the butter. Add the sugar then the beaten eggs and flour and lastly the fruit. Bake for 4 hours.

Quaker Oat Biscuits

¼ lb margarine
¼ lb sugar

2 tablespoons golden syrup
1 small teaspoon almond essence

Mix together in a pan. Add ½ lb Quaker oats. Butter a dripping tin. Spread the mixture in, and bake in a cool oven, one hour. Cut into fingers when cold.

Queen Cakes

1 lb flour
¾ lb butter (cream it)
¾ lb caster sugar
¾ lb currants
8 eggs
2 teaspoonfuls baking powder

Queen Cakes II

½ lb butter beaten to a cream
½ lb sugar
¾ lb flour
6 oz currants
4 eggs
Flavour to taste
An egg less may be used and a teaspoonful of baking powder added in its place.

Rock Buns

½ lb flour
¼ lb sugar
1 teaspoon baking powder
A very little milk
¼ lb butter and lard mixed
1 egg

Rolled Gingerbread

¼ lb raw sugar
4 oz butter
3 oz treacle
Ginger to taste
Also a few drops of essence of lemon

Mix altogether after having melted the butter and treacle, then drop the mixture on a well greased tin. Bake in a moderate oven. When nearly cold it may be either rolled over a ruler or cut in squares; to be kept in a tin in a dry place.

Royale Icing

Whites of 2 eggs
Icing sugar
A little lemon juice
A very little blue colouring

Pass the sugar through a fine sieve, and keep adding it to the whites until the mixture will not drop off the spoon.

Sandwich Cake

Whisk 4 eggs for five minutes, add gradually:
½ lb caster sugar then:
Nearly ½ lb ground rice
A tablespoonful of flour
1 teaspoonful of baking powder.

Whisk well. The same will do for ground rice cake or buns.

Sandwich Cake II

¼ lb butter
¼ lb sugar
¼ lb flour
2 oz ground rice

4 eggs
1 teaspoonful baking powder

Seed Cake

½ lb butter
½ lb eggs
½ lb sugar
½ lb flour
½ lb ground rice
1 oz seeds

Seed Cake II

6 oz butter
12 oz flour
2 eggs
Nutmeg
½ lb sugar
¾ tumbler milk
Seed
2 teaspoonfuls baking powder

Shrewsbury Cake

½ lb butter
½ lb sugar
1 lb flour
2 eggs

Roll very thin and cut.

Soda Cakes (x4)

1 lb flour, rub in
¼ lb butter
½ lb caster sugar

½ lb currants or sultanas
2 eggs
2 teaspoons baking powder

Flavour with grated lemon. Mix with one gill of milk. Bake in a moderate oven in 4 teacake tins.

Sponge Cake or Swiss Roll

¾ lb loaf sugar
½ teacup of water

Boil together until they come to a syrup. Pour boiling on to 7 eggs leaving, out the whites of three. The eggs must be beaten 5 minutes before pouring on the sugar, and 20 minutes after pouring the sugar on. Then add ½ lb of flour, stirring well into the mixture. Bake in a moderate oven. For Swiss Roll bake in a dripping tin lined with paper. Take paper off whilst hot. Spread on raspberry jam and roll up in a cloth and sprinkle sugar on it - 2 cakes - or 1 cake and Swiss roll.

St George's Hall Cake

½ lb flour
2 ½ oz sugar
1 oz candied peel
1 egg
3 oz dripping or lard
1 oz currants or sultanas
1 oz ginger
1 ½ teaspoon baking powder

Milk to mix to a slack consistency. Bake in a moderate oven.

Sultana Cake

¼ lb butter
¼ lb castor sugar

¼ lb flour
¼ lb sultanas
2 eggs
A very little finely chopped candied peel

Work the butter to a cream. Then add the sugar and work for about 10 minutes. Then break in the eggs one by one. Mix well and beat for 5 minutes. Then add the flour and stir in lightly the fruit and bake in a moderate oven for ¾ of an hour.

Sultana Cakes II

½ lb butter
½ lb caster sugar
¼ lb flour
10 oz sultanas
2 oz sweet almonds
¼ lb candied peel
5 eggs

Beat butter to a cream with sugar. Add the eggs one by one and beat well. Mix in dry ingredients. Blanch and chop almonds, putting part in the cake and laying 2 or 3 cut in half on the top. Bake from 1 ½ to 2 hours in a moderate oven, or if desired can be baked in pastry tins, or small cake tins. Leaving out the white of one egg and adding a little baking powder is sometimes considered an improvement.

Tea Biscuits

1 egg
½ lb of flour
¼ lb of butter
6 oz of sugar
A pinch of salt
2 teaspoonfuls of baking powder

Rub the butter into the flour. Add the sugar, then salt and baking powder. Beat the egg well, add it and mix into a stiff paste not using any water. Roll it well with the hands on the board until first smooth. Roll out very thin and cut into rounds or fancy biscuits. Put on a cold baking sheet and bake in a moderate oven until a light brown.

Tea Cakes

2 lbs flour
5 or 6 oz butter
1 tablespoonful sifted sugar
1 teaspoonful salt

Set the sponge with one third of the flour and half an oz yeast to ferment for two hours. Then add the remainder of the flour. Warm the butter and mix altogether and beat for half and hour into a stiff paste.

Tennis Cake

¼ lb butter
¼ lb sugar
5 oz flour
1 oz ground almonds
3 oz cherries (cut one cherry in four)
2 eggs
½ teaspoonful of baking powder

Beat the butter to a cream. To decorate mix almonds and pistachios together, chopped finely and decorate the edge with almond icing.

Toasted Plum Cake

1 lb flour
¾ lb sugar
½ lb butter (or lard and margarine)
2 teaspoons of baking powder
2 gills milk (lukewarm)
1 oz yeast
1 oz currants

A little candied peel and nutmeg

Warm the milk and put yeast in to rise. Beat butter and sugar to a cream, add milk and yeast. Mix in all the other ingredients in dry. Bake about 3 hours, put into three 1 lb bread tins.

Vienna Icing

3 oz butter
6 oz sugar
A few drops of carmine and a little vanilla

Beat butter to a cream. Add sugar gradually then flavouring, divide the icing, colouring one half pink. Now put the mixture into a piping bag, putting the white on one side, and the pink on the other. The icing will come pink and white.

Walnut or Almond Cake

¼ lb butter
¼ lb castor sugar
5 oz flour
3 eggs
½ teaspoon of baking powder
1 ½ oz crushed walnuts or almonds

Beat butter to a cream, add sugar, mix well together. Then put in the beaten eggs, adding gradually. Lastly flour, baking powder and almonds. Mix well, turn the cake into a tin lined with paper and bake in a moderate oven, about 40 minutes. When the cake is cold, split it into two or three and spread with almond or walnut mixture. Put the pieces together again and cover with water icing.

Walnut or almond mixture

About 3 oz crushed walnuts or almonds
3 oz icing sugar
About half the white of an egg

Mix sugar and almonds together then add the beaten white of egg and make a paste. Put on the layers of cake. Jam together and cover with water icing.

War Loaf

2 cups brown sugar
2 cups hot water
2 tablespoons lard or dripping
1 lb seedless raisins or sultanas
1 teaspoonful salt
½ teaspoonful cinnamon

Boil all together 15 minutes. When cold add 3 capfuls of flour, 1 teaspoon baking soda dissolved in 1 teaspoon hot water. Bake in two cakes in moderate oven for 45 minutes.

Welsh Cake

1 breakfast cup of flour
¾ teacup sugar
4 oz butter
1 egg
2 teaspoons baking powder

A little salt - currants and lemon - and milk to make the above into a batter. Well butter a flat tin and bake in a quick oven for 15 to 20 minutes.

Welsh Cake II

¼ lb butter
¼ lb castor sugar
¼ lb flour
2 eggs
3 oz currants
1 oz glace cherries

2 oz almonds (blanched and split)

Whisk butter to a cream then add sugar and beat for 5 minutes. Then break in eggs one at a time and beat again for 5 minutes. Mix in lightly the flour and currants and the cherries cut up in small pieces. Bake in a flat tin for 20 minutes. When the cake is well set in the oven, sprinkle all over it the split almonds.

White Gingerbread

1 lb flour
½ lb butter
½ lb white sugar
¾ oz ground ginger
A teaspoonful baking powder
A little milk

Rub the butter into the flour and add the other ingredients

Breads and Tea Breads

Cheese bread

Made like a bread and butter pudding with slices of cheese or grated cheese.

Currant Bread or Cake

1 lb flour
1 lb sugar
1 lb currants
½ lb butter (or margarine)
¼ lb peel
¾ oz yeast
1 gill warm milk
2 eggs
1 tablespoon baking powder

Rub the butter into flour. Crumble the yeast in, then mix altogether and put it into the tins and set down to rise ½ hour by the fire. Will make 3 small cakes.

Currant Bread II

1 ½ lb flour
1 ½ oz margarine
1 oz yeast
4 oz sultanas
4 oz currants
4 oz sugar
1 ½ oz peel
1 egg
Milk (warm) to mix
A little salt

Rub the margarine into the flour. Add the rest of the ingredients. Beat the egg and mix with the warmed milk.

Spoon Bread

1 cup of corn meal, sprinkle into a pint of milk and leave for 15 minutes to curdle. Put in 4 yolks of eggs well beaten, a cup of boiled rice cold. Now whip the 4 whites and stir carefully and bake about 20 minutes in a soufflé dish and serve with chicken.

Chutneys, Pickles, Relishes, Jams, Jellies

Apricot or Plum Jam

To each 4 lb of fruit allow 4 lb of sugar and ½ a pint of water.

Put sugar and water into the preserving pan. Stir until moistened and warm. Add fruit and boil briskly about 20 minutes then put into jars and cover.

The apricots must be peeled and sprinkled with some of the sugar to drain out the juice.

Aspic Jelly

2 lb knuckle of veal or thin beef
2 quarts of water
A bouquet of herbs, thyme, parsley and bay leaf
1 carrot
1 small turnip
1 onion

Cut up the beef or veal and place it in a pan with the water. Bring to a boil. Skin, now add the beef and flavourings and simmer for 5 hours. Strain through a hair sieve and when cold remove fat.

Jelly: take one quart of stock and place it in a pan. Add salt and pepper, 1 ½ oz of gelatine. Stir until quite melted. Whisk up the whites of 3 eggs to a stiff froth and whisk into the jelly with 2 tablespoons of tarragon vinegar. Bring to a boil. Boil 5 minutes. Let it stand a few minutes, then strain through a clear towel well rinsed in hot water.

Bramble Jelly

1lb of brambles
2lb of apples

To every pound of fruit allow 1 pint of cold water. Boil well and strain twice. Weigh the juice then boil quickly (to reduce) for 20 minutes. Then add 2 lbs of sugar for 3 lbs of juice. Stir until the sugar is dissolved and boil quickly for about 20 minutes.

Bramble Jelly II

To 10 lbs brambles and
3 lb apples

Allow 10 pints of water. Boil well and strain twice. Then boil quickly for 20 or 30 minutes to reduce them. Then measure, and to every pint of juice allow ¾ lb lump sugar and boil quickly for about 20 minutes or until it jellies.

Calves Foot Jelly

1 ½ pint stock
½ pint sherry
10 oz loaf sugar
3 lemons
1 wine glass of brandy
3 whites of eggs

Prepare the stock by the former recipe for calves foot jelly stock. Remove the fat from the top carefully and place in a pan with the lemon rind, and sugar. Stir until the sugar is dissolved. Add sherry and the whites of the eggs whisked to a stiff froth, and lemon juice. Whisk in well, and bring to a boil. Cook for 7 minutes and strain through a jelly bag.

N.B. discretion must be used in the quantity of wine used, as if the stock is very strong jelly, more might be added. To simmer it, sometimes it is advisable to add a very small quantity of gelatine.

Calves Foot Jelly Stock

Take 2 calves feet which should be scalded and broken by the butcher. Just cover them with cold water, bring to a boil. Throw away the water and mash in clear cold water. Now place in a pan and pour onto them 3 pints of cold water. Bring to a boil, and simmer gently with the pan lid on for about 5 hours. These should be about 1½ pints at the end of the time. Strain through a clean hair sieve and let the stock get quite cold.

N.B. if the stock is not reduced sufficiently at the end of 5 hours it must go on cooking.

Chutney

2 quarts of vinegar
4 quarts green gooseberries, stewed and pulped through a sieve
½ lb moist sugar
¼ lb salt
2 oz garlic
2 oz ground ginger
2 oz mustard
2 oz turmeric
2 nutmegs grated

Boil all together for twenty minutes and when cold bottle. Rhubarb will do quite as well.

Dried Apricot Jam

1 lb dried apricots
1 oz bitter almonds
6 gills water
3 lbs sugar

Cut apricots fine and soak 48 hours. Place in a pan and boil until it sets. 2 ½ lbs sugar will do, if boiled longer.

Green Tomato Pickle

Slice one gallon of green tomatoes. Put a handful of salt to each layer of tomatoes. Let them stand for 12 hours. Strain off the juice and throw it away. Add 2 green pepper corns and from 2 to 4 onions, sliced. Take 2 quarts of strong vinegar. A little more than ½ pint treacle, 2 tablespoons whole mustard, 1 teaspoon allspice and cloves. Set on the fire and when it begins to boil add the tomatoes and onions. Let it boil for 10 minutes. Put the mixture in a stone jar, fasten down tight and put in a cool place. Ready in a fortnight but greatly improved if kept for longer.

Marmalade

1 dozen Seville oranges
1 sweet orange
2 lemons

Rub the oranges with salt to clear the skins. Cut up the oranges finely, taking out the seeds only. To one pound of shred fruit, add three pints of water. Let this stand all night to next day. Boil till tender. Let it stand again all night, then to every pound of fruit, add 1 ¼ lbs of sugar to boil till transparent. Be sure and cut out all the white part of the lemons, as it does not boil transparent.

Marmalade II

20 Seville oranges
4 sweet oranges
2 lemons
9 lbs of sugar

Boil ½ an hour, quickly the first time and ¾ of an hour the second time.

Marrow and Apple Jam

7 lbs of marrow
3 lbs of apples
6 oz of sugar
1 ½ oz of ground ginger

Rind and juice of 2 lemons. Cut the marrow into small pieces. Pit and core the apples. Put all into a basin and let the sugar and ginger and lemons all be well stirred and stand 24 hours. Time to boil: about ½ hour.

Marrow Jam

Peel and remove the seeds of marrow. Cut into pieces 1 inch square. Put on a dish and strew over a little brown sugar. Leave until next day. Allow one pound of sugar to each pound of marrow, also 1 ½ oz of whole ginger (bruised), the rind of 2 lemons and the juice of 3 to every 4 lbs of marrow. Boil until the marrow is clear and transparent. 1 drachm of chillies improves it. Stand the marrow in a sunny window 3 or 4 weeks to dry up the sap and then they make a much better preserve. 2 oz of ginger allow to 6 lbs of marrow. 1 drachm, is a ¼ of a ¼ of an oz.

Orange Marmalade

The fruit must be sliced very thin all together, only picking out the pips. Quantity in a boiling:

3lbs of oranges
4 ½ quarts of water
10 ½ lbs sugar
The juice only of 4 sweet oranges

After cutting up, pour over the water and let it stand for 24 hours - and then boil without this sugar for 1 hour quickly. After it comes to the boil let it stand 24 hours and then boil with the sugar, 1 hour quickly.

Orange Marmalade II

12 Seville Oranges
4 lemons
4 Sweet Oranges

Slice the fruit as fine as possible. Peel the rind off the oranges and then throw away the white pith. Allow to stand 24 hours. Add 3 pints of cold water to each pound of fruit, then boil until tender. Leave it until next day, boil till clear with 1 ¼ lb of sugar to each lb of fruit. It will jelly when ready. Boil quickly.

Orange Marmalade III

3 sweet oranges
12 Seville oranges
2 lemons

To each pound of sliced fruit add 3 pints of cold water and let the whole stand 24 hours. Then boil until the chips are tender and leave it until the next day. To each pound of boiled fruit add 1 ¼ lbs of loaf sugar and boil till the syrup jellies (quickly).

Pickled Damsons

4 quarts damsons are 8 lb
2 quarts damsons are 4 lb
1 pint vinegar
1 ¾ lb loaf sugar
10 cloves

Tick or prick the damsons with a silver fork. Put them into a large pan. Boil the vinegar, sugar and clove together. Pour over the damsons. Let them stand 24 hours then drain off the syrup or boil it or pour over the damsons. Then let them stand another 24 hours covered closely. Then put the damsons with the syrup into a preserving jar and let them simmer 10 minutes after coming to a simmer. Then put them into jars and cover closely. When cold tie down with bladder.

Preserve Butter in Brine

4 oz salt

1 oz lump sugar
1 oz saltpetre
6 quarts cold water

Boil all together for 20 minutes. When cold put in butter wrapped in cloth.

Preserved Cherries

¾ lb sugar to 1 lb cherries weighed after being stoned. Boil quickly for an hour and quarter.

Raspberry and Red Currant Jam

Take 3 lbs of red currants. Add to them 1 quart of cold water. Bring to the boil. Simmer for a few minutes then strain through a hair sieve. Get all the juice, but don't rub the pulp through. Allow ¾ of a lb of sugar to a pint of juice. Put the juice back into the pan, and add 8 lbs of raspberries, allowing ¾ of a lb of sugar to each lb of fruit, boil quickly. Boil the juice and fruit together for a minute or two, then add the sugar and boil quickly.

Raspberry Jam

3 ½ lbs red currants
3 pints of cold water

Bring to the boil and simmer for a few minutes. Then strain through a hair sieve. To each pint of juice, put ¾ lb of sugar. Put the juice back in the pan. Add 1 lb raspberries and 1 breakfast cup of cold water. Boil it up together. Then add the sugar, and boil quickly to keep the colour. Allow ¾ lb of sugar to each pound of fruit.

Raspberry Vinegar

To 6 pints of raspberries put 3 pints of vinegar. Let them stand in a stone jar for 24 hours, stirring frequently with a wooden spoon. Put

6 lbs of loaf sugar in an earthen pot and your raspberries in a sieve and let them drop into the sugar. When done dropping, put it into a preserving jar. Over a clear fire, let it simmer, taking the skin off as it rises. When it begins to boil take it off the fire, and put it in a bowl to cool. Then bottle. Do not squeeze the fruit, or the syrup will be thick.

Red Currant Jelly

Put the currants into a pan and cover with cold water. Boil quickly until the first is well cooked. Strain twice, then to 1 pint of juice allow ¾ lb of loaf sugar, and boil quickly until it will jelly, about 20 minutes.

Red Currant Jelly II

Drain the juice from the currants without stripping them and to 1 pint of juice allow 1 lb fine granulated sugar which has been made hot in the oven until quite brown. Pour the cold syrup over the sugar and stir till dissolved.

Rhubarb Jam

3 lb rhubarb
1 lemon
3 lb lump sugar
1 oz bitter almonds

Cut rhubarb small. Blanch and chop fine the almonds. Put all into a bowl to stand 12 hours. Strain off syrup and boil 20 minutes. Then add fruit and juice of lemon, again boil 20 minutes without stirring so as not to break the fruit.

To Bottle Fruit

Fill wide necked bottles with the fruit wanted, and into each bottle, put ¼ lb of fine castor sugar. Shake the fruit well into the bottles as they require filling, as light as possible. Tie each bottle over with a bladder and put them into a pan with enough cold water, to come to the neck of the bottles, which must be packed well round with hay, to prevent the bottles touching each other. Let them fist come to the boil and then take the pan from the fire. Leave the bottled fruit in the pan till the water is quite cold. If the fruit is not very juicy ½ lb sugar is better.

To Pickle a Tongue

½ teaspoonful saltpetre
3 tablespoonfuls Demerara sugar

Rub in plenty of salt and leave covered with salt. Turn and taste every day for 3 weeks.

To Preserve Plums

1 pint of water
5 lbs of lump sugar to 6 lbs of big plums

Put water and sugar on to slow fire and stir occasionally until sugar is dissolved. Whilst this is being done prepare plums. Place them in a bowl and cover with boiling water for one minute. Pour hot water off plums and run cold water on, this will enable the peel to come off. Then add plums to syrups and simmer all for about 1 hour, or until plums look clean and turn pink or red. If any plums should be hard to peel put them again in hot water for a minute.

Tomato Chutney Sauce

6 lbs ripe tomatoes
3 lbs sour cooking apples
4 oz salt
8 oz brown sugar
3 pints vinegar
6 cloves of garlic
6 oz ground ginger

1 oz mustard seed

Scald the tomatoes. Remove the skins. Cut them into slices and put them into an earthenware cooking pot with the vinegar, salt and apples previously peeled, cored and chopped finely. When the fruit is soft rub the whole through a sieve. Add the sugar, ginger and mustard seed, also the garlic (chopped finely) and boil the whole gently from ½ to ¾ of an hour.

Pour the contents of the cooking pot into a jar. Cover it and let it stand in a warm place for about 3 days. Then bottle the chutney for use. Lock up tightly and exclude the air. Time 3 days.

Tomato Marmalade

3 lbs tomatoes
3 lbs sugar
2 lemons

Pare the lemons very thin and put in very small pieces. Squeeze out the juice. Skin the tomatoes and put all the ingredients into a preserving pan. Boil about 1 hour, keeping it constantly stirred.

Walnuts Pickled

Get the walnuts in July. Prick them well with a large needle or steel fork. Then put into salt water for a week, changing it every three days. Then put into the air to turn black. Make a pickle for them. 1 lb salt to 3 quarts of water.

Wine Jelly

1 ½ pints of water
½ pint sherry
3 lemons
¾ lb loaf sugar
Whites of 3 eggs
1 ½ oz gelatine (Marshall's)

1 wine glass brandy

Soak the gelatine in cold water until soft. Place water, gelatine, thinly pared lemon rind and sugar in a pan. Stir until the gelatine is melted. Now add the wine and strained lemon juice and whisked whites of eggs. Whisk whites well in. Bring to a boil, boil 5 minutes then allow to stand 2 minutes and strain through a jelly bag well rinsed in hot water. When quite clear add brandy.

Sauces, creams, seasonings, dressings

Batter for Fritters

2 tablespoonfuls of flour
½ tablespoon salad oil
1 egg
Wineglass of warm water
A little salt

Put the flour into a basin. Add oil, water, salt and yolk of egg. Stir all together. Stand ½ an hour. Add the whipped white of egg and use at once.

Cough mixture

1 oz sweet nitre
½ oz squills
¼ oz Ipecacuhana

Cream

Sixpenny jar of cream (add a little milk)
1 oz caster sugar
¼ oz gelatine dissolved

Whisk cream for a short time. Add the sugar and then the gelatine. Flavour to taste and then mould and set in a cool place.

Curry sauce

½ pint stock
1 onion
½ an apple
Juice of ½ a lemon
½ tablespoon curry powder
1 ½ oz dripping (or any other fat)

1 tablespoon of curry paste (if liked)
½ oz flour
½ teaspoon sugar
Seasoning

Chop the onion and apple. Fry in powder paste, flour, fat, seasoning for 15 minutes. Add the rest.

Frying batter

2 oz flour
½ or ¼ pint of lukewarm water
1 egg
½ tablespoon salad oil
¼ teaspoon salt

Place flour in a basin. Add yolk of egg, oil and salt to it. Stir water into them. Let them stand ½ an hour. Whisk white of egg to a stiff froth. Stir lightly into the mixture and it is ready.

German Sauce

Yolk of 1 egg
½ tablespoon castor sugar
½ pint of sherry

Whisk all over the fire in a pan until first warm and quite frothy. Pour around the pudding. Be careful not to cook sauce too much or it will curdle.

Hollandaise Sauce

2 tablespoons vinegar
2 tablespoons of water
Yolks of 2 or 3 eggs
Salt and pepper
2 oz butter

Boil vinegar and water together for 2 or 3 minutes. Place in a jar with half the butter and seasoning and after just breaking up the yolks of the egg add those. Stir this in a pan of boiling water until it begins to thicken, then add the remainder of the butter.

Horseradish Sauce

½ a stick of horseradish
1 tablespoonful of vinegar
2 tablespoonfuls of cream
A little salt and mustard

Mayonnaise Salad Dressing

Yolk of 2 eggs
6 tablespoonfuls salad oil
3 tablespoonfuls of vinegar
chilli and tarragon can be used
Salt and white pepper to taste
1 tablespoonful white stock
2 tablespoonfuls of cream

Beat the yolk very smoothly. Add the oil very slowly, stirring well all the time with a wooden spoon. This is the secret of having a smooth sauce: mix in the vinegar, add the stock and then the cream. Keep constantly stirring and keep in a cool place then bottle and keep lightly corked.

Mayonnaise Sauce

2 oz butter
2 eggs (yolks)
1 teaspoonful of mustard
1 teaspoonful castor sugar
½ teaspoonful salt and pepper mixed
4 tablespoonfuls vinegar
2 tablespoonfuls cream

Melt further in a basin and sit in a pan of hot water. Then mix with the yolks (off the fire). Add sugar, mustard, pepper and salt. Stir well into the butter and eggs then drop the vinegar in a few drops at a time. Stir gently all the time. Put the basin back into the pan of water on the fire and stir until it thickens. When cold add the cream. Very good when salad oil is objected to.

Prepared Seasoning

White pepper 2 oz
Black pepper ¾ lb
Nutmegs 2 oz
Cloves ¼ oz
Salt 4 oz
Jamaica pepper 2 oz
Cayenne pepper 1 oz
Mace 1 oz

All finely powdered and mixed.

Salad Dressing

Yolks of 2 hard boiled eggs
1 teaspoon of salt
1 teaspoon of mustard
1 teaspoon of castor sugar
2 tablespoons of vinegar
½ pint of cream

Rub the yolks with the other ingredients to a fine paste. Add vinegar and then the cream.

Salad Dressing II

Boil one egg for ten minutes, then take out the yolk, and bind it with ½ a teaspoonful of salt. Add to it 1 teaspoonful of dry mustard. 2 teaspoons of vinegar, 2 tablespoons of cream. Stir well together. Strain through a sieve.

Salad Sauce

Take the yolks of two eggs. Add pepper, salt and mustard and salad oil one drop at a time. Work with wooden spoon till quite stiff then add tarragon and Chile vinegar and a little cream. It is then ready for use.

Seasoning for Pork Pies

To 3 lbs meat:
1 oz salt
½ oz pepper (black)
½ teaspoonful ground mace
A prick of cayenne pepper

Tartare Sauce

Take the yolks of 4 eggs and stir them in a basin for a few minutes. And then drop in salad oil till the mixture is quite thick. Stir for about 10 minutes and then mix in gradually 1 teaspoonful chilli vinegar, the same quantity of tarragon vinegar, ½ teaspoonful of finely chopped capers and 1 teaspoonful of the vinegar from a bottle of capers and season nicely with salt and pepper.

Tomato Sauce

Break up a pound of ripe tomatoes. Put in a saucepan with a salt-spoonful of salt and sugar, a morsel of onion, a tiny sprig of thyme and parsley, a tablespoonful of minced bacon and a couple of ounces of butter. Cook them, giving an occasional shake, until they can be passed through a hair sieve. Take care to press all through and scrape under the sieve. Repeat it. Add a few drops of carmine and a little cayenne pepper.

Tomato Sauce II

Put 12 medium sized tomatoes into a pan with 1 pint of vinegar. Cut up the tomatoes. Add:

A little cayenne pepper
2 teaspoonfuls of ground ginger
2 tablespoonfuls of sugar
2 cloves of garlic

Boil all well for ½ an hour. Strain and bottle.

Tomato Sauce III

A breakfast cup of small tomatoes
½ oz butter
1 small onion sliced finely
2 tablespoons stock
1 teaspoonful cornflour
Salt and pepper

Put all the things except the cornflour into a pan and simmer for 10 minutes. Now strain. Thicken with the flour. Return to the pan and stir until it boils and it is ready for use.

Veloute Sauce

1 oz butter
1oz flour
¼ pint white stock
¼ pint milk or cream
A little salt

Melt the butter in a pan and add the flour. Now put in the stock and cream. Mix until they boil. Cook well and add salt.

Whip Sauce

Put the yolks of 2 eggs, and the white of 1 egg into a basin

One tablespoon castor sugar
One glass sherry
One tablespoon lemon juice

Put the basin into a pan that is half full of boiling water, and whisk until stiff and frothy.

Whipped Egg Sauce

1 egg
1 tablespoonful caster sugar
1 tablespoonful of water

Put into a jug which will stand in a pan of hot water and whisk until a stiff froth. Nice for Castle Puddings. Nicely flavoured with sherry.

White Sauce

1 oz butter
1 oz flour
¼ pint strong stock
¼ pint cream and milk
Salt to taste
2 tablespoons of aspic jelly

Melt the butter in a pan. Add the flour, then the stock and milk or cream. Stir over the fire until it boils. Cook well, add aspic, seasoning the sauce, and when cool it is ready.

**Recipes mentioned by title but without ingredients or cooking instructions were:

Orange Cream, Apricot Cream, Lemon Cream, Chartreuse of Pineapple or fresh Plum, Strawberry Cream, Chocolate Cream, Coffee Cream, Caramel Cream, Jamaica Cream, Velvet Cream

Drinks

Boston Cream

Boil 1 galloon of water with 3 lb of brown sugar for 20 minutes. When cold add the whites of 3 eggs, ¼ lb tartaric acid and 3 oz essence of lemon. Mix and bottle. To make the drink, pour 1 tumbler of cold water into a wine glass full of the mixture and about ¼ teaspoonful of carbonate soda.

Coffee

1 oz coffee to 1 pint water
2 earthenware jugs, both thoroughly heated

Place in one of them an oz of coffee and add one pint boiling water. Let it soak for 2 minutes. Then stir well and allow to stand 3 minutes. Pour it all into the other warm jug.

Fruit Salts

2 oz carbonate soda
2 oz cream of tartar
2 oz tartaric acid
2 oz bicarbonate soda
2 oz epsom salts
1 oz magnesia
4 oz powdered loaf sugar

Dry each ingredient separately. Roll them well, mix altogether. Put into bottles for use, keeping each quite air tight.

Dose - 2 teaspoonfuls in half a tumbler of water - what is found suitable.

Ginger Beer

1 lb sugar to each gallon of water
1 lemon to be sliced and squeezed
1 oz bruised ginger

The water to be poured over the ingredients, boiling and closely covered. When lukewarm, a little yeast to be put on a crust and added to it, and left to ferment for 36 hours. To be carefully strained and bottled.

Ginger Cordial

4 drams of essence of ginger
2 drams of capsicum
3 teaspoons of tartaric acid
2 ½ lbs of loaf sugar

Dissolve sugar and acid in 1 quart of boiling water. When cold add the other ingredients. Stir well and bottle, then add water as desired. Especially good with soda water.

Lemonade

Rind of 3 lemons, juice of 3 lemons
1 gallon water boiling
1 lb loaf sugar

Lemonade II

8 lemons (juice)
1 lemon rind
¾ lb lump sugar
3 pints of water
½ teaspoonful of cream of tartar
White of one egg

Lemonade III

Juice of 8 lemons
Rind of 1 lemon
¾ lb of lump sugar
8 pints of water

Index

List of contributors:

Mrs Watson, Mrs Wilson, and Miss Barnes; buildings or locations: Burnholme, Goathland, Beech House, Moorlyn, Sunhill; individuals (all female as we would expect from the era) Miss J Daniel, Mrs Herbert, Mrs Channon, Mrs Davison, Mrs Carr, Mrs Buchanan, Miss Clay, Miss Maples, Mrs Sutheran, Mrs Bishop, Mrs Johnson,

Mrs Terry, Mrs Claxton, Mrs Glaisby, Miss A Hirt, Mrs White, Mrs Hutchinson, Mrs Harwood. Mrs Spink, Nurse Robinson, Mrs K William, Mrs Scotson, Mrs Bruce, Miss Farrar, Mrs Gladys Low, Mrs Stringer, Mrs Lauden, and Mrs Love.

Made in the USA
San Bernardino, CA
08 September 2017